THE KIPLINGER WASHINGTON LETTER

THE KIPLINGER WASHINGTON EDITORS
1729 H St., NW, Washington, DC 20006-39

Dear Client:

   <u>The workplace...it's a-changing, and it will change even more</u> in the years ahead as different types of jobs require whole new skills. You will have to adjust to this in your own business and line of work. So will your children and grandchildren as they think about the future.
   You may want to pass this Letter along to them for some ideas.

   <u>People will have to take more responsibility for their careers</u>... assessing their strengths & weaknesses, planning schooling and job paths. The days are gone when just about anyone could step into a lifetime job with regular pay raises, promotions and a good pension at retirement.
   <u>They'll have to be skilled in something</u> that the market needs, such as sales, mechanics, finance, teaching, computers or health care. Those without something to offer will have a hard time making a living.
   <u>Constant upgrading and retraining</u> will be needed by most workers. They'll have to understand the entire business, not just their own jobs.

   <u>There will be more outsourcing</u>, contracting out some functions to other companies...bookkeeping, payroll preparation, food service, etc. In Manhattan, one firm now handles mailroom operations for 60 clients.
   <u>Lets employers stick to their core business</u>, what they do best. Nike, for example, concentrates on marketing its shoes and clothing... contracting out all of its manufacturing to 500 plants around the world.

   <u>Temps, part-timers and contract workers will be added as needed</u>, complementing a smaller number of full-time, long-term company employees.
   <u>Giving managers maximum flexibility</u> in keeping their payrolls low during slack periods and then adding staff quickly when orders increase.
   <u>Also leased employees</u> to work wherever the company may need them, with the lessor handling payroll and taxes, benefits and other rigmarole.
   <u>Means less job security</u> for many workers and often less loyalty. Most employers WANT to provide security, but they can't be more generous than the marketplace allows. That's why honing a skill is so important. If your job becomes unnecessary, it won't be enough to be a hard worker. You'll need a marketable skill that you can take from company to company.

   <u>Those who work on sharpening their talents will do all right</u>. In a downturn, managers will try hard to hang on to their best employees. If skilled workers lose their jobs, they'll be the first hired elsewhere.

   <u>Ability to work as part of a team will be essential</u> to success as companies rely on their people to go beyond their narrow specialties. A lab scientist with a good idea will work on it with other scientists, then with production and marketing teams, bringing the idea to fruition.
   <u>There will be less top-down management</u>...pyramids of bosses and subordinates. Instead, many workers will be organized into teams, making decisions on how to do jobs, hiring, firing and other matters.

Technology will revolutionize the workplace in the years ahead.

Computers will make it more democratic...top execs communicating directly with workers down the line, lessening need for middle managers.

Millions of additional people will work from their own homes, dealing with their co-workers, customers and suppliers by computer.

Others will work out of satellite offices, cubicles rented out near their homes, equipped with computers, printers, phones and faxes.

Hundreds of uses of new electronics: Screening job applications. Conducting interviews by teleconference. Designing and testing products with 3-D computers. Electronically searching through computer files by voice commands. And technology to help disabled people on the job... just wink an eye or speak into a microphone to start sending a message.

Productivity advances too. Using new technology, an Ala. plant makes more steel with 3000 workers than it did 30 years ago with 30,000.

New portable phone/computers will make communications easier. You will be able to contact customers or employees WHEREVER they may be. Orders, bills and other communications will be transmitted by satellite.

People will work together without even being in the same country. In the future, simultaneous engineering of complex plans will be common by sharing computer files...design teams in different parts of the world working on the same projects, using the latest three-dimensional visuals.

Jobs in the same company will be scattered throughout the world. Orders handled in Singapore. Accounting in Germany. Management in U.S.

U.S. will create nearly 14 million jobs in the next ten years... a slower pace than the past decade. Manufacturing jobs will edge down, from 17% of all jobs now to 12% by 2005 and probably below 8% by 2015. Many manufacturing jobs are evolving into service-type occupations... engineering design, systems integration, data processing and others.

An older workforce, baby boomers reaching middle age and beyond. The median age of workers will advance from 38 now to about 41 by 2005.

Expect fewer early retirements. More people will work to 65-70. As we live longer and healthier lives, we'll remain on the job longer.

The Hispanic share of the workforce will increase 25% by 2010. Asians, around 50%. Black percentage will stay about the same. Minorities will keep moving up the corporate ladder in the next 15 years. Managers who know how to deal with a diverse workforce will have an edge.

Lots of opportunities for women. They now own a third of firms in the U.S. Look for women to run more retail and service-type companies and advance even more rapidly in construction, engineering and other jobs traditionally held by men. Gender barriers will continue to disappear.

Women will hold about HALF of all jobs, up from the current 46%.

Metro areas that will add the most jobs over the next 15 years, based on projections by NPA Data Services, a Wash., D.C., research firm:

Atlanta	903,600	Los Angeles	699,500
Houston	834,100	Orange County, Calif.	616,600
Wash., D.C.	734,100	Seattle	599,200
Dallas	730,600	San Diego	590,100
Phoenix	720,800	Tampa-St. Petersburg	531,200

Best job prospects in these lines, which will grow fast in the coming years:

Computer specialties of all sorts, including systems designers, engineers, systems analysts, repair technicians, programmers and electronic paginators, who create layouts for desktop publishing.

Health care, such as paramedics, physical and occupational therapists, radiology specialists, dental hygienists, speech pathologists, medical assistants, pharmacists, ophthalmologists, opticians, medical records keepers, drug researchers.

Care for elderly will be provided by a variety of businesses with staffs of residential counselors, therapists, doctors, nurses, home health care people and home-care aides to meet their needs.

Jobs in education will increase due to a growing population under age 17. There will be strong demand for teachers of math, science, special ed, preschool and English as a second language.

Fastest-Growing Jobs Now to 2005	
Home-care aides	119%
Home health aides	102%
Systems analysts	92%
Computer engineers	90%
Physical therapy aides	83%
Electronic paginators	83%
Occupational therapy aides	82%
Physical therapists	80%
Residential counselors	76%
Human services workers	75%
Occupational therapists	72%
Cosmetologists	69%
Medical assistants	59%
Paralegals	58%
Medical records keepers	56%

(Source: Bureau of Labor Statistics)

Business will need financial specialists, accountants, brokers, marketing and ad people. And always openings for topflight salespeople.

Law...copyright, bankruptcy and health attorneys plus paralegals.

Recreation, entertainment and leisure-time activities will offer plenty of job opportunities in everything from travel and sporting goods to time-share resorts, health clubs and the film and music industries.

Science. Plenty of demand for engineers, biologists, chemists, meteorologists and others who know their stuff. Mostly at smaller firms.

And good blue-collar jobs for those who learn a specialty... heating/air conditioning, plumbing, carpentry, bricklaying, auto repair.

Young people should start with a solid education. It'll pay off. A strong liberal-arts background is the foundation for future training. Median pay for college grads is $37,300. For high school grads, $23,970. Over a lifetime of work, the college grad will earn about $600,000 more.

And then specialize in something. There won't be much demand for generalists with no particular skills, nothing special to offer.

At the same time, they must be flexible. Graduates in accounting or engineering may end up in marketing or management. Be open to change.

Communications skills are a MUST, getting ideas across clearly.

For a rundown on a wide array of jobs and their prospects...

Get "Occupational Outlook Handbook" by Labor Dep't specialists. Costs $32 from Sup't of Docs., Box 371954, Pittsburgh, Pa. 15250-7954. Be sure to mention stock number 029-001-03220-0. Or phone 312-353-1880. The information is free on Internet, "http://stats.bls.gov/ocohome.htm".

Education will be a lifetime process, not just 12-16 years or so. Employers will sponsor refresher or upgrade courses at community colleges or at the workplace. Some will put courses right on a worker's computer.

Schools will have to adapt to the demands of global competition.

Work-study programs will expand...students dividing their day between school and jobs, where they develop good skills and work habits. There will be apprenticeships in such fields as computer programming and drafting, graphic arts, cooking, electronics, mechanics and welding. Industries will set standards for grads who want to qualify for jobs.

Expect more emphasis on entrepreneurship at business schools... practical courses on financing, sizing up markets, selling and managing, the kind of knowledge young people must know to actually run a business.

Unions will target gov't workers, immigrants, teachers, doctors, emphasizing they're in no position to get a fair shake without a union.

But membership won't rise much, remaining near 16% of all workers and 11% of the private workforce. Reasons...fewer manufacturing jobs, stiff global competition and problems organizing in the South and West.

Pay will be tied more to performance of individual employees. More emphasis on incentive bonuses for meeting specific job goals... less on year-after-year salary increases that push base pay sky-high. A lot of talk nowadays about pay disparity between high and low-incomers. But U.S. employers CAN'T pay unskilled workers more and compete globally.

Trend will be to fixed benefit costs, shifting more of the risk to employees in terms of deductibles, co-payments and other expenses. Another trend will be to tighten up on benefits offered to retirees.

The move to 401(k)s will continue, transferring pension risks to employees, many of whom have no background for investment decisions. Fewer companies will stick with traditional defined-benefit pensions, leaving many people in the dark on the income they'll have at retirement.

There's concern workers aren't saving enough for their future. Biggest job growth is at small firms, many of which don't offer pensions.

Congress will step in, change individual retirement account rules to make it easier for people to put aside a little extra for retirement. It will probably OK higher income limits for deducting IRA contributions. Eventually, it'll also make sure the social security fund doesn't go dry, probably by raising retirement age and reducing cost-of-living increases.

Opportunities for those starting careers will be better than ever. U.S. business is in the best competitive position it has been in years, offering a wide array of promising careers for young people to choose from. Now it's up to them to provide the expertise and gumption employers want.

Yours very truly,

Knight Kiplinger   *Austin Kiplinger*

THE KIPLINGER WASHINGTON EDITORS

P.S. A few words to our younger readers, especially students:
You'll live and work in a world of many cultures and languages. There will be new forms of global commerce we can't even imagine today. Opportunities and options in American business will grow astronomically. You will be challenged in the years ahead to retain the best of the old while at the same time accepting and adjusting to international horizons.
We're confident that you're up to the job. Good luck.

THE COMPLETE JOB SEARCH ORGANIZER 1997-'98

THE COMPLETE JOB SEARCH ORGANIZER 1997-'98

HOW TO GET A GREAT JOB—FAST

BY JACK O'BRIEN

KIPLINGER
TIMES BUSINESS

RANDOM HOUSE

**KIPLINGER
BOOKS**

Published by
The Kiplinger Washington Editors, Inc.
1729 H Street, N.W.
Washington, D.C. 20006

Library of Congress Cataloging-in-Publication Data
O'Brien, Jack, 1936-
    The complete job search organizer : how to get a great job—fast /
by Jack O'Brien. — 3rd ed.
        p. cm.
    "A Kiplinger book."
    Includes index.
    ISBN 0-8129-2931-4
    1. Job hunting. I. Title.
HF5382.7.0268 1997
650.14—dc21   97-2871
                                                                                CIP

This publication is intended to provide guidance in regard to the subject matter covered. It is sold with the understanding that the author and publisher are not herein engaged in rendering legal, accounting, tax or other professional services. If such services are required, professional assistance should be sought.

9 8 7 6 5 4 3 2
Third edition. Printed in the United States of America.

Book designed by S. Laird Jenkins Corp.
Original drawings by Fred Moore.

Sources for notes in margins: National Association of Colleges and Employers; the National Center for Education Statistics, U.S. Department of Education; *Occupational Outlook Quarterly,* a publication of the U.S. Department of Labor, Bureau of Labor Statistics; and the *Current Biography Yearbook.*

DEDICATION

I dedicate this book to my grandchildren—Kara, Kristen, Joseph, Karleigh, Sean and Riley—with love and affection, and hope that they may live their dreams.

PREFACE

This book evolved from letters of advice I wrote to my children as they approached college graduation. I believed that changes in the work world would require me to update the book about every three years. Now, to be current, an annual update is mandatory.

Three dynamic factors have transformed today's job market since I first wrote this book. First, our economy is driven by technology and technology-related services. Second, the Internet has changed the way we communicate, access information and distribute knowledge. Third, as companies downsize, rightsize, and reinvent themselves, good job performance is no longer a guarantee of continued employment. This means lower-priced recent graduates with marketable skills (technical, writing, speaking and people) enjoy a bright employment picture. But to stay competitive, you need to continually improve your skills and develop new ones.

So, this edition includes new material on the job-market outlook, the use of online services in your job campaign, and how to develop and improve your marketable skills, at your leisure, from your home or office. I hope this just-in-time information will help you get quick employment in an interesting field and a good return on your college investment.

Some things don't change. This book focuses on the whole process of landing your dream job, in as brief and direct a way as possible. You can accept, reject, or modify my advice. After all, your life and your choices are your own. But please keep in mind that my advice reflects years of hiring, coaching and observing young people develop and prosper in the business world.

As you flip through the pages, you will realize that this is more than just another job-search book. You will find many easy-to-use forms and checklists. They are intended to help you think, plan and plot your job campaign by encouraging you to write things down—on paper or in your computer. They are also intended to help you arrange your activities into manageable tasks—that is, organize yourself.

Finally, this book will help you motivate yourself to take action, to get you started in your job campaign, to *just do it!* When you do something, you get a reaction, and other things start to happen. Soon, you build momentum. And, before you know it, you have an offer for the job you want. It is that simple. But it is not that easy. You have to work at it. The harder you work, the more likely you will succeed at getting your dream job.

Every book requires a team effort. This one reflects the commitment of David Harrison, Director of Kiplinger Books, who believed in my concept. I was introduced to David by his assistant Dianne Olsufka, who also proofread the book. This book depended upon the endorsement of Knight Kiplinger, Editor in Chief of *Kiplinger's Personal Finance Magazine.* It benefited from the initial interest in my work by Jack Kiesner, Editorial Director of the *Kiplinger Washington Letter,* who was introduced to me by Dick Golden, my friend and retired *Letter* editor.

My editor, Pat Mertz Esswein, deserves unlimited credit and thanks. She has really gotten into this book as a work in progress and continues to help me say what I mean to say.

This book has evolved from the early help of my former assistant Carol Lloyd. Also, I am indebted to John Birdsong, my former business partner, who exposed me to the blessings and curses of the Internet. This book benefits from the talent of Fred Moore, a college senior when he drew the illustrations, who used the book to land his first post-college job. Thanks also to Karmela Lejarde, who researched the interesting margin items; Jennifer Cliff O'Donnell, who researched the job-market overview; and publicist Jennifer Robinson.

I thank my family for their love, humor, inspiration and motivation—especially that of my lovely wife Barbara—to share my thoughts with you.

Jack O'Brien, Washington, D.C.

CONTENTS

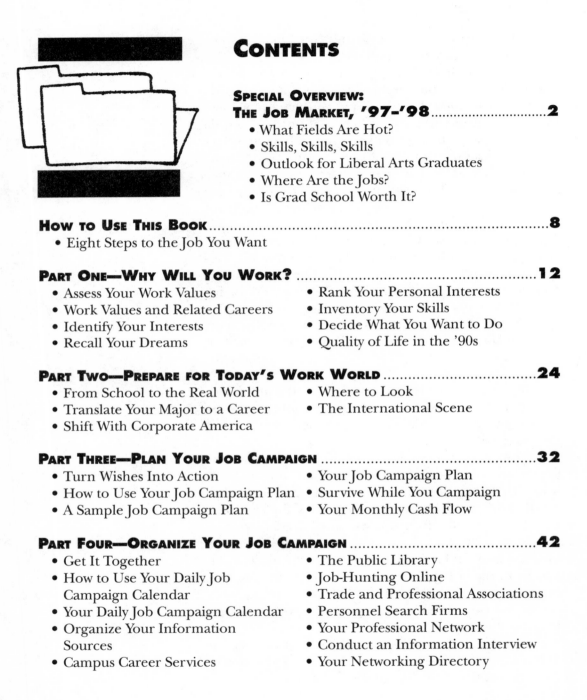

CONTENTS

INTRODUCTION

By Knight A. Kiplinger
Editor in Chief, *Kiplinger's Personal Finance Magazine*

Over the years I have talked with many young men and women embarking on their first serious job hunts. They come to me while "networking," and they're looking for specific leads they can follow up. Whether or not I can help them with that, I try to give them something more...my ideas on what makes a first job valuable. I'd like to share these thoughts with you, too, as you set out on this adventure.

What you should seek in your first job isn't the best pay, or job security, or even a clear upward path within that particular company. The best starting jobs are ones in which you'll be:

- **worked very hard** by managers with high standards,

- **taught up-to-date, transferrable skills,** and

- **given a chance** to show your worth.

Your first few jobs should be résumé builders, the kinds of jobs in which you'll learn skills to use for the rest of your life, even if you change jobs or careers several times.

A job like that will be so valuable that the pay should be irrelevant. *You* could pay your *employer* for the privilege of working there, and it would still be a bargain for you. If your first few jobs meet these tests (and you do, too), then your later jobs will come easily.

We at the Kiplinger organization are proud to publish this fine job-search guide by Jack O'Brien. The readers of our periodicals are successful managers, business owners and professional people. They read our *Kiplinger Letters* for judgment on where the economy is headed and how government actions will affect their work. They read *Kiplinger's Personal Finance Magazine* for advice on managing their own money. Our readers are people who understand that, as my grandfather W.M. Kiplinger said, "The times will always be changing. Much of life and work consists of looking for the changes in advance and figuring out what to do about them." That's a practical and proven approach for all times, bad or good.

That's why you should persist in looking for the opportunity you want, regardless of what's said about the economy, the job market, or the outlook for a degree, graduating class, or generation. With the help of your education, your hard work, and a reasonable degree of luck, anything is possible. This book will show you how to put them all together. If you achieve the kind of results you're capable of, we look forward to serving your information needs, too, in a few years.

Best wishes and good luck!

Knight Kiplinger

Washington, D.C.

THE JOB MARKET, '97-'98

WHAT FIELDS ARE HOT?

Recent college graduates couldn't have picked a better time to enter the workforce. Although corporate downsizing continues, experts agree that entry-level positions for both liberal arts and business graduates are out there for anyone willing to do a little legwork.

After an absence of several years from the job market, large corporations are hiring again, boosted by increases in sales and profits. Small and midsized companies are continuing to pop up throughout the country, many of them looking for entry-level employees who are willing to grow with the business.

Of course, some fields are hotter than others with home health care, criminal justice and computer engineering leading the way. But traditional jobs are also in demand, said Marv Roth, director of career services at Lafayette College in Easton, Pennsylvania. "The service and consulting fields are good right now," said Roth. "There's also a lot of activity in accounting, sales and management development."

As a newly minted or reinvented graduate, you should keep two points in mind:

- **First, today's job market is driven by information** which in turn is driven by technology and technology-related products and services. Regardless of your field of interest, you must be computer-literate. Computer skills are a minimum requirement now and into the coming century.

- **Second, your competitive edge in any job market is that you provide HELP!**, that is, **H**igh **E**nergy and **L**ow **P**rice. It is sometimes appropriate for a company to replace an ineffective person making $50,000 a year with two recent graduates making $25,000 per year.

Top Ten Skills Employers Want

In descending order:

Good oral communication skills or presentation skills

Interpersonal skills

Teamwork skills

Analytical skills, problem solving and critical thinking

Flexibility or cross-functional skills

Leadership skills

Written communication skills

Proficiency in field of study or industry-specific skills

Computer knowledge

Hands-on experience, such as an internship or cooperative education

Source: University of North Carolina at Wilmington

SKILLS, SKILLS, SKILLS

Companies are adopting a back-to-basics policy when evaluating college graduates, placing an emphasis on interpersonal and leadership skills and good oral and written presentation skills. Graduates entering specific professions such as accounting, law or education will still have to demonstrate knowledge and competence in their field, but more than that, they'll have to prove they are well-rounded.

The University of North Carolina at Wilmington polled hundreds of companies on what they were *really* looking for in a new hire. The results showed that companies desire candidates with good interpersonal skills more than those with specialized educations. See the accompanying list of the top ten "hot skills" as compiled by the university.

Experts say the trend toward hiring well-balanced applicants is the result of the ever-changing business environment. "We want employees who can problem solve, who are willing to be flexible and grow with the company," said Jill Taylor-Sullivan, director of human resources with the Rockport Company in Marlboro, Massachusetts. "Job definition lines are more blurred than they have been in the past. More and more you're seeing companies offer exciting opportunities to employees, but those opportunities are open only to people who are flexible."

Today's graduate must demonstrate leadership skills as well as an ability to go with the flow. "It doesn't matter where you hone your leadership skills—with a fraternity, a church group or through athletics," said C. Randall Powell, director of placement at the Indiana University School of Business. "[You can get by without] some of the cognitive skills if you can prove you're a leader."

But good interpersonal skills still aren't enough to land a job. Every job-hunting graduate must have computer skills, say the experts, especially liberal arts graduates. "You can't have enough computer skills," said Marv Roth. "Not just in the computer field but across the board. A liberal arts background with computer skills is a strong background."

Computer skills in demand today include knowledge of spreadsheet programs like *Excel* and *Lotus 1-2-3*, word processing programs and Windows, and the ability to navigate the Internet and World Wide Web and to retrieve and send e-mail.

No matter what your major is, you can boost your chances of employment by landing an internship or cooperative work-study program while still in school.

Hot Fields for 1997 Business & Science Grads

Computer information systems (CIS)
Accounting
Engineering
Finance
Health care

THE OUTLOOK FOR LIBERAL ARTS GRADUATES

Liberal arts graduates needn't feel intimidated by this year's job market. For years, it appeared only business graduates had a shot at landing a job right out of college, but the tide has turned in favor of the well-rounded student. "From what we've seen, the outlook for liberal arts graduates is very good," said Lynda Garow, director of career services at Clark University, in Worcester, Mass. "Liberal arts graduates are sought after for their critical thinking, problem solving, communication and flexibility, as well as for having diverse and global perspectives."

To increase their competitiveness, all liberal arts graduates need to demonstrate computer fluency and flaunt any technological experience. Camille McKinley, editor of the *CAM Report* (Career Advancement and Movement), advises liberal arts graduates to highlight foreign language ability. "Foreign language is becoming important for businesses. There's a real need for people who can speak Spanish, Japanese, French and German," said McKinley.

WHERE ARE THE JOBS?

The Northeast and Northwest aren't the job hot spots they used to be, but big cities like New York, Boston and Seattle shouldn't be ruled out by job hunters. Large corporations are hiring again due to a friendly business economy and the sheer number of jobs available in big cities are evident by the thickness of their newspapers' Sunday Classifieds.

Communities in the Southeast and the Midwest look good for '97 and '98 as businesses pop up to support the region's growing populations. For a list of the 20 cities with top job growth, see page 30.

Still, career counselors believe new graduates might have better luck in their hometown or a smaller city where start-up and small or midsized companies need employees to grow with the business.

Fastest Growing Occupations, 1994–2005

Between 1994 and 2005, according to the U.S. Bureau of Labor Statistics, the U.S. workforce will increase by 17.7 million jobs. Many of those positions are expected to come from burgeoning fields like health care and computer technology. (Note: If you're graduating with a college degree, you may be overqualified for a personal, home-care, or home-health aide position, but plenty of companies will be in the business of hiring, placing and managing aides, and that's where a job might await you, especially if you have business, human service or nursing skills.)

	Percent Change		Percent Change
Personal and home care aides	119%	Residential counselors	76%
Home health aides	102	Human services workers	75
Systems analysts	92	Occupational therapists	72
Computer engineers	90	Medical Assistants	59
Physical and corrective therapy aides	83	Paralegal	58
Electronic pagination systems workers	83	Medical records technicians	56
Occupational therapy assistants and aides	82	Teachers, special education	53
		Correction officers	51
Physical therapists	80	Operations research analysts	50

Source: U.S. Department of Labor, Bureau of Labor Statistics

Is Grad School Worth It?

Hot Fields for 1997 Liberal Arts Grads

Sales
Customer support
Law (paralegal)
Special education
Criminal justice

That depends on your goal. Clearly, if you're entering a field like accounting, engineering or education, a Master's degree might not just be a good idea but a requirement for any job you seek. But if you're thinking about graduate school because you didn't get the job offer you wanted or because you want to avoid the workforce for a few years, then you're probably wasting your time and your money.

"For entry-level employees, it's a bad idea," said Jenny Duffey, owner of Duffey Communications, a public relations firm in Atlanta. "Real experience is the master, more than education. Save graduate school until you know what you might want to specialize in in your chosen profession."

There are other reasons to enter the job market before tackling graduate school, said C. Randall Powell, director of placement for Indiana University's School of Business. "Some graduate schools require a few years of work experience. Besides, if you go to work first, the company you end up working for might even help pay to send you to graduate school," he said.

If you're afraid that holding off on your Master's degree might prevent you from ever going back to school, fear not. "There is a strong record in this country of people going back to school," said Powell. (For more on this, see the discussion of virtual campuses beginning on page 148.)

So, bottom line, you should only go to graduate school if you can make this statement: "This is what I want to do and I need a graduate degree to do it."

How to Use This Book

Congratulations, you have made an important decision in acquiring *The Complete Job Search Organizer*. Its action-oriented contents will help you be more productive and successful as you compete for the job you have dreamed about and launch your career.

What makes this book special?

For starters, it's more than a book. It is a planner and organizer aimed at designing your personal game plan and coaching you through your career development and job campaign.

Who should use The Complete Job Search Organizer?

College students, recent graduates and graduate students will find this guide to be helpful, as well as those whose first or second jobs turned out to be false starts or dead ends.

Why should you use it?

You need this book to land a job that provides the rewards you expect from your college investment.

When should you begin your planning and organizing?

If you're a college student, you could begin using *The Complete Job Search Organizer* after your freshman year. It could help influence your choice of major, internships and summer jobs. If you are a college junior, senior or recent graduate, this guide is just in time to help. Even if you are a college graduate in a low-wage or dead-end position, you can still use it to reinvent your career.

Eight Steps to the Job You Want

The *Complete Job Search Organizer* is a no-nonsense, hands-on tool for getting the job you really want. To get the most out of it, read the book once through completely. This will help you appreciate how helpful the forms and worksheets will be in planning and organizing your job campaign. Then invest in a good three-ring binder or create a directory and set up the necessary computer files—either system will eventually become your personal job-search organizer. Go through the book again, but follow all the instructions and do all the exercises in each section. Each section represents one step—or tactic—on the way to landing the job that is a good fit for you and your skills.

Why Will You Work?

Part One helps you identify your work values, interests and skills. The exercises will help you determine what kind of career matches your strengths, needs and future goals.

Prepare for Today's Work World

Part Two shows you where to find today's jobs. Evaluate the prospects for your career based on the information you find in Part Two.

Plan Your Job Campaign

Part Three provides forms and worksheets that lead you through the job campaign process and offers tips on surviving financially during your job search.

Organize Your Job Campaign

Part Four helps you arrange your job campaign activities into manageable tasks. It also teaches you where to find valuable information that can help you make intelligent career decisions.

Ben Nighthorse Campbell, U.S. senator from Colorado, graduated from San Jose State University with a double major in physical education and fine arts. His first job was teaching art and shop at an elementary school.

Job Offers By Major

The percentage of job offers by area of study made to 1996 graduates:

Business	**39.2%**
Engineering	**31.9%**
Computer sciences	**7.9%**
Humanities and social sciences	**7.7%**
Sciences (including math)	**3.5%**
Education	**2.8%**
Health sciences	**2.7%**
Communications	**2.6%**
Agriculture and natural resources	**1.2%**
Home economics	**<1.0%**

When You Market Yourself

Part Five shows you how to present, promote, position and price yourself in today's job market.

Job Campaign Tactics That Work

Part Six offers suggestions for competing for the job you want. You can also learn how to outwit and outmaneuver your job competitors.

Interview for First Place

In Part Seven, you learn the art of persuading your prospective employer that you are the best qualified candidate for the job.

Time to Make a Decision

Part Eight shows you how to gracefully accept or decline a job offer. By working through the "Job Offer Evaluation" worksheet, you can decide whether this job is the one for you. It also offers advice for success in your new career.

Five Important Points Before You Begin

1. **Research will be a big part of your job campaign strategy**—the more you know, the better able you will be to compete for the job you want. Throughout *The Complete Job Search Organizer,* you will find discussions of how to research your options, career fields, companies or prospective employers. For example, in Part Four, "Organizing Your Job Campaign," you will be introduced to resources such as the public library, trade and professional organizations, and electronic information services. Remember to use all your resources to their fullest potential.

2. **The key to converting this book to your personal game plan is to write things down.** By putting your thoughts in writing, you transform theory into reality. You make probable what was previously only possible. In addition, you start a process that makes things

happen. Then, you'll have something to react to. The result is a game plan that will work for you.

3. **You provide the self-motivation.** Many of us have the desire to win. Fewer have the will to out-prepare, out-think and out-work our competition. But that is what makes us winners. *The Complete Job Search Organizer* provides the techniques and advice you need to compete successfully for your dream job. But it's up to you to add positive attitude and persistence to your job campaign.

4. **This book will help with your record keeping** by providing the following worksheets as well as suggestions on how to use them for best results. Look for the "copy" insignia that identifies each one.

- Work Value Assessment (page 15)
- Dreams and Personal Interests (page 17)
- Skills Inventory (page 18–19)
- Job Campaign Plan (page 36)
- Monthly Cash Flow (page 41)
- Daily Job Campaign Calendar (page 45)
- Networking Directory (page 71)
- Résumé Checklist (page 79)
- Action Log (page 89)
- Job Prospect Profile (page 106–107)
- Job Campaign Improvement Suggestions (page 135)
- Job Offer Evaluation (page 139)

5. **Create your personal job-search organizing notebook** by reproducing all of the forms and placing them in a three-ring binder with tabs or recreating them on your personal computer. This makes it convenient to add information as you progress in your job campaign and easier to locate the information you need when you need it. Remember, if you do the right things right, you will succeed in your job campaign.

Jean Auel, author of Clan of the Cave Bear, earned a master's degree in business administration while working full-time as a circuit-board designer at an electronics firm.

PART

ONE

WHY WILL YOU WORK?

ASSESS YOUR WORK VALUES

Work is a key element of our existence, in every phase of our development. We work to realize our dreams, develop our potential, and obtain the material goods we need to survive and prosper. Work lets us contribute productively to our families, communities and our world. Through work, we can fulfill a mission.

To make proper career choices, you must place the acquisition of material and nonmaterial wealth in proper balance from your own perspective. You might call this balancing your checkbook with your values. The question you have to answer is "What do I want to be?" rather than, "What do I want to have?" When you know what motivates you, you can then begin to make career decisions with more satisfying results. Use the following list of work values and related careers to help you think about and assess your work values. This list isn't intended to be all inclusive. However, it will help you get started. This is the beginning of a lifelong process. Every job you take on will help you refine or expand your thinking. Good luck!

Work Values and Related Careers

Work Value	Related Career
Accomplish much	Any job can be done with pride!
Achieve self-fulfillment	See the worksheet on the following page.
Achieve financial security	Own your own business
Build	Architecture, catering, construction, sculpting
Be physically active	Any work outdoors, health and fitness instruction and administration, natural resources management, professional sports
Care for the earth	Agriculture, conservation, forestry service, geology, marine biology, nonprofit activism, politics
Create	Design. Any job!
Direct/lead others	Education, management, military service
Feed the world	Agriculture, animal husbandry, private volunteer organizations
Gain experience	Any job!
Gain fame	Radio, television, theater, philanthropy, politics
Help others	Health services, missionary service, nursing home administration, social services, special education, Peace Corps
Improve society	Education, law enforcement, medicine, nonprofit foundations, religion
Make money	Any job!
Meet others	Hotel and restaurant management, politics, promotion, sales, tourism
Serve the public	Education, government, law enforcement, social services
Share knowledge	Education, religion, research, writing
Stimulate my intellect	Library administration, publishing, research of any kind, university education and administration
Travel	Airlines, diplomatic service, importing and exporting, international business, missionary work, politics, travel arranging, wholesale business
Use new technology	Computer systems management, industry, invention, medicine, science, space exploration
Work at home	Anything using computers, crafts and sewing, day care
Work independently	Consulting of any kind, fine arts, freelance writing, freelance photography, research

Work Value Assessment

Now start thinking about your work values. Fill in the spaces below with the top five to ten work values you believe are most important to you, including any that were not on our list of examples, and describe why they're important to you.

You may wish to discuss this exercise with someone who knows you well and can give you objective input, such as your roommate,

professor or close friend.

Don't worry, there aren't any "correct" answers. This exercise is simply meant to help you know yourself better. Chances are the results don't surprise you, but now you have a valuable profile of yourself on paper that you can refer to again. Compare this list with your interest list, which follows.

Important Work Values   *Why They're Important to Me*

1. _____   _____

2. _____   _____

3. _____   _____

4. _____   _____

5. _____   _____

6. _____   _____

7. _____   _____

8. _____   _____

9. _____   _____

10. _____   _____

Identify Your Interests

Successful people don't realize they're working because they are having too much fun. They sometimes exceed their own potential because they are so passionate about what they are doing. So, if you want to be happy in your work, find something that is important to your well-being and that you can do passionately. Combining what you love with what you need is an important key to success. The following sample links passions to careers possibilities.

Passion	*Career*
Art	Cultural activities, education, fine arts, gallery management, museum administration
Children	Day care, elementary education
Clothes	Fashion design, fashion merchandising, retailing, sewing, tailoring
Crafts	Clothing or home furnishings design and construction, graphic design, interior design
Creativity	Advertising, architecture, catering, desktop publishing, marketing
The disabled	Physical therapy, special education, social work
The elderly	Health care, nursing home administration
The environment	Air, water or waste management, manufacturing process management, natural resources and wildlife management, nonprofit activism
Food	Catering, cooking, food service, food writing, institutional nutrition, restaurant management
Games	Computer systems, product testing, retailing
Money	Banking, commissioned sales, investing
Music	Artist promotion and management, entertainment, radio production and management
The outdoors	Botany, construction, forestry, parks and recreation, U.S. Park Service
Physical activity	Aerobics, agriculture, coaching and training, dance instruction
Problem-solving	Customer service, management, medicine, politics, science, any job!
Reading	Editorial services, education, library science, publishing, research
Sports	Coaching and training, leisure events, professional athletics
Technology	Industry, science, telecommunications
Travel	Photography, tour operation, writing
Travel overseas	Importing and exporting, military service, Peace Corps

Recall Your Dreams

You can convert your dreams to reality, but first you have to dream: What have you always wished that you could do? Imagine yourself in your dream job: What are you doing? Where? Why? How? Don't put any limits on your imagination—start here and add as many pages as you need to your job-search organizing notebook to accommodate your vision. Try it!

_____

_____

_____

_____

_____

_____

Rank Your Personal Interests

Based on the results of the preceding exercises, go back and rank your top five to ten personal interests by priority.

1. _____

2. _____

3. _____

4. _____

5. _____

6. _____

7. _____

8. _____

9. _____

10. _____

Take Inventory of Your Career-Related Skills

To make a successful career choice, you must match your interests with your skills. Career-counseling services at local universities and community colleges often offer career testing: interest, aptitude and personality tests. Interest tests translate your likes and dislikes into relevant vocational options. Aptitude tests reveal your ability to do certain types of work well. Personality tests provide information about characteristics that make you suitable for a particular occupation. While these tests do not add up to one prescribed course of action, they are usually very helpful in determining your strengths, weaknesses, likes and dislikes, and in evaluating career options. They are also an objective way to confirm your own hunches, and the value of the information generally exceeds the reasonable costs.

In the meantime, use the quick self-assessment below to get you started. Identify your relevant skills in each category, citing a specific example. These skills are not job-specific. As with all the lists in this book, this list is a starting point. You can expand it or limit it as you choose.

Category	Career-Related Skill	Your Specific Skill
Communication	Write well	_____
	Speak effectively	_____
	Speak a foreign language fluently	_____
Critical thinking	Identify issues	_____
	Analyze options	_____
	Create solutions	_____
Computer literacy	Know word processing programs	_____
	Know spreadsheet programs	_____
	Know graphics programs	_____
Leadership	Set the example	_____
	Coach others	_____
	Guide a group	_____
Management	Set goals	_____
	Establish priorities	_____
	Manage time and money	_____
Human relations	Be a team player	_____
	Fulfill commitments	_____
	Respect other opinions	_____
Interpersonal	Follow instructions	_____
	Build skills	_____
	Use common sense	_____

Career-Related Skills Inventory and Development

Skills Inventory

Using the results of the preceding exercise as a basis, now rank your top five to ten skills in order of your personal proficiency.

1. _____
2. _____
3. _____
4. _____
5. _____
6. _____
7. _____
8. _____
9. _____
10. _____

Skills Development

Now, write down the skills, in order of preference, that you would most like to develop.

1. _____
2. _____
3. _____
4. _____
5. _____
6. _____
7. _____
8. _____
9. _____
10. _____

Most Popular Majors Among Males by Race

White
Business and
  management   24%
Social sciences   14%
Engineering   9%

Black
Business and
  management   26%
Social sciences   15%
Engineering   6%

Hispanic
Business and
  management   23%
Social sciences   16%
Engineering   9%

Asian/Pacific Island
Business and
  management   21%
Engineering   20%
Social sciences   11%

**American Indian/
Alaskan Native**
Business and
  management   18%
Social sciences   15%
Education   8%

DECIDE WHAT YOU WANT TO DO

Having assessed your work values, dreamed your dreams and identified your interests and inventoried your skills, you should now have a good idea of what you do or do not want to be. Once you know what you want to be, deciding what you want to do is easy. However, all of us do not get to this milestone prior to our first attempt at a career. Some of us have to experience a career first, then make changes based upon what we have learned. This trial and error method is a valid approach because we learn from experience. However, we want to avoid obvious career mismatches as much as possible. The following five suitability questions may help prevent you from starting off in the wrong direction.

Five Career Suitability Questions

1. **Would I stay in this career if I didn't get paid for a period of time?** This "love versus money" question may be the real litmus test of what you want to do.

2. **Do I want to spend the next three to five years working in this career?** This will be the average length of a career in the early twenty-first century.

3. **Am I comfortable with the people in this field?** If you can't relate to the people involved, you probably don't belong here.

4. **What is the future for this career?** There are few opportunities in a dead-end career.

5. **What can I contribute over time?** Visualize your role and responsibilities in this field three to five years from now.

You will have to find your own answers to these questions. There are no approved solutions. However, just thinking about these issues should provide a clearer focus of what might be best for you.

Use some of the following publications to research your options and find out about available and appropriate careers. You may also want to interview experts in various career fields prior to reaching any firm conclusions. (For more about information interviews, see Part Four, page 66.)

Suggested Reading

- *Build Your Own Rainbow*
  Barrie Hopson and Mike Scally, Pfeiffer & Co.

- *Dreams Into Action*
  Milton Katselas, Dove Books

- *The New Quick Job-Hunting Map*
  Richard Nelson Bolles, Ten Speed Press

Suggested Career Software

If you have access to an IBM-compatible personal computer, the following software can be very helpful. Both programs act as automated mentors for self-directed career- and job-search assistance.

- *Career Design*
  Career Design Software
  800–346–8007

- *DBM's Job Lander*
  Drake Beam Morin, Inc., New York
  800–345–JOBS

Most Popular Majors Among Females by Race

White	
Business and management	17%
Education	15%
Health professions	10%
Black	
Business and management	23%
Social sciences	11%
Education	9%
Hispanic	
Business and management	19%
Social sciences	12%
Psychology	9%
Asian/Pacific Island	
Business and management	24%
Social sciences	11%
Life sciences	10%
American Indian/ Alaskan Native	
Business and management	16%
Education	15%
Social sciences	11%

QUALITY OF LIFE IN THE '90s

While money is a critical factor in your job/career decisions, the opportunity for personal growth and how you spend your free time are equally important. No amount of money can make up for having the wrong job in the wrong place at the wrong time. Here are five guidelines for evaluating the quality of life as it relates to your career.

Experience

There is no substitute for experience. Sometimes it is necessary to accept a low-level job in your field of choice in order to gain entry and acquire valuable experience.

Lifetime learning

Education and personal growth are more closely related than most people realize. To make yourself more marketable, you need to build your skills every day. Company-sponsored training programs as well as company-paid educational opportunities are critical for career advancement. To make yourself and your life more interesting, take classes for fun—not grades.

Recreation

Opportunities for leisure activities are important to prevent personal doldrums, dullness and burn-out. We all need to refresh our minds and bodies for the daily challenges of the workplace.

Location

Many of today's jobs are location-independent and you may have more choices of where to locate. Don't rule out smaller or medium-size cities; many offer a quality cultural scene without big city prices or hassles.

Affordable living

If all of your money goes toward housing and commuting, you won't have much left for the fun things. Be able to live within your means.

Considering these work-related issues will help you lead a happier and more productive life, regardless of your career choice.

By now you should know more about yourself and the direction you want to take with your career. The information you have gained will be helpful in writing your résumé, networking and interviewing. Each of those activities is an important element in any job campaign, and each is discussed in detail in this guide.

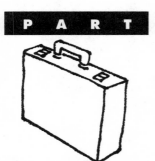

P A R T

T W O

PREPARE FOR TODAY'S WORK WORLD

FROM SCHOOL TO THE REAL WORLD

Schoolbook learning and career success are not necessarily related. In school, you learn to learn. At work, you apply learning to a purpose. School learning is an individual effort. In the work environment, teamwork is essential. In school, tools such as computers are usually banned during examinations. At work, one can hardly survive without a computer. In many school settings, you read and listen to lectures. In the world of work, you learn from experience. To make the transition from school to work, consider taking courses in the following subjects, while still in school or after.

- **Business communications,** to learn how to write and speak in the business world.

- **Computer literacy,** to learn how to use at least one word processing, one spreadsheet and one database or desktop publishing application.

- **Interpersonal skills,** to help you work more easily and effectively with others.

- **Business-economics and finance,** to understand the financial and economic impact of business decisions in the world of work.

- **New career tools,** to equip you with, for example, a foreign language or accounting skills.

- **Your passion,** to make you even more knowledgeable about it.

Suggested Reading

- *The Best Jobs for the 1990s and into the 21st Century*
Ronald and Caryl Krannich, PhD's, Impact Publications

Robert Johnson, founder and chairman of Black Entertainment Television, originally aspired to a career in foreign service. He placed sixth in his class at the Woodrow Wilson School of Public and International Affairs at Princeton.

A Word for Liberal Arts Majors

If you are a liberal arts major questioning the value of your degree in today's work world, relax. You are well-educated. Now you need to transfer your personal skills into the workplace and develop new job-specific skills. If you want to become a manager, you must be willing to develop basic skills first—learn from the ground up. Look for paralegal, research assistant or

Match Your Major to a Career

If you have made a decision regarding your college major prior to thinking about your chosen career, the following list may help link your college major to a career. Compare your major to your work values, interests and skills identified in Part One, "Why Will You Work?" Look for a consistent pattern or tendency that will point you toward the right career for you.

College Major	Career Field	College Major	Career Field
Art	Architecture	**English**	Church work
	Computer graphics		Desktop publishing
	Decorating and design		Information systems
	Gallery management		management
	Media production		Journalism
			Law
Business	Accounting and finance		Library management
	Administration and		Management
	management		Mediation and arbitration
	International trade		Paralegal services
	Manufacturing		Publishing
	Marketing and sales		Teaching
			Technical writing
Communications	Advertising		
	Market research	**Health sciences**	Insurance
	Media management		Medical administration
	Mediation and arbitration		Physical therapy
	Public relations		Public health agencies
	Publishing		Radiological technology
			Teaching
Economics	Financial services		
	Government	**Journalism**	Advertising
	research and service		Books, newspapers,
	The nonprofit sector		magazines
	Trade associations		Information systems
			management
			Law

administrative assistant jobs, where your reading, analytical and writing abilities can be utilized. Become computer literate. Ideally, find an employer that offers a training program or a mentor who can teach you the workplace skills you need. If you are a people person, look for work in sales or customer service. Above all, view your liberal arts education as an advantage—because it gives you a strong base upon which to build.

College Major	Career Field	College Major	Career Field
Journalism (cont'd.)	Library management	Political science and government	Diplomatic service
	Market research		Government service
	Mediation and arbitration		Land use planning
	Publishing		Law
	Teaching		Politics
	Trade associations		Trade associations
			Transportation
Languages	Church or missionary work		
	Customer service	Psychology	Advertising
	Diplomatic service		Clinical research and services
	Human and social services		Market research
	Importing and exporting		Public relations
	Law enforcement		Sales
	Peace Corps		
	Publishing	Recreation	City and county programs
	Telecommunications		Event planning
	Tour operations		Hospitality services
Mathematics/ sciences	Architecture		Resort management
	Computer programming and software design		Theme park activities
	Engineering		Travel and tourism
	Environmental services	Social sciences	Advertising
	Manufacturing		Government service
	Military service		Market research and planning
	Research and development		The nonprofit sector
	Systems analysis		Paralegal services
	Teaching		Philanthropic foundations
Music	Church work		Public relations
	Entertainment		
	Instrument sales		
	Publishing		
	Teaching		

Pharmacy Wins

Prospective employers in 1996 offered the highest average salary—$49,248 —to undergrads earning bachelor's degrees in pharmacy.

SHIFT WITH CORPORATE AMERICA

Most new jobs will come from smaller-growing companies with fewer than 500 employees, not large, restructuring companies. And, many of the new jobs will be in midsize areas (cities with less than 500,000 population) rather than in major urban centers.

To identify growing companies, follow this three-step procedure:

1. **Choose the type of employer and/or geographic location you desire.**

2. **Based on this criteria, search the following resources** to target organizations of interest to you.

3. **Call or write each targeted firm's public relations, marketing or public information office** to obtain an annual report, product and/or service information, organization charts, and the names and titles of key people to contact. An annual report will tell you if the firm is growing and profitable. It typically provides a history of growth, successes, new products and/or services and financial status. Many times it includes an outlook for the next year. Some privately owned companies probably won't publish an annual report, so ask for a press kit instead.

Information Sources

There are numerous sources of information about organizations. They include the following:

Directories

Geographic, business, occupational, professional, industry and financial directories are available in your public library. These directories provide information about an organization's products and/or services, number of employees, principal executives, annual revenues, and location(s). (See also Part Four, "Organize Your Job Campaign.")

Trade associations

These organizations produce membership directories, journals and newsletters and hold conferences that may serve your networking purposes. Almost every field or industry is affiliated with a trade association. (See page 61.)

Newspapers

The business section of most newspapers contains numerous articles about local companies and their activities. Look for new-product announcements, executive promotions (for key names) and notices of corporate expansions. Also, keep up with news, trends and government activity, and scan the society pages for potential contacts.

Online information services

These services allow you not only to research corporate information, but to use résumé data bases and electronic classifieds and to network electronically (see pages 57 and 68). They're an interesting way to make your job search more extensive, provided you either have the necessary equipment—a personal computer, modem and access software—or can use it at a library, parent's office or a business-service center, such as Kinko's. You'll also need the know-how to use these tools without frustration and potentially excessive costs.

Last—Not Least

Prospective employers in 1996 offered the lowest average salary—$18,654 —to students earning their bachelor's degrees in pre-elementary education.

20 Cities With Top Job Growth in 1996–1997

For detailed information regarding any of these areas, write the local Chamber of Commerce in each city. In order of greatest growth:

Atlanta

Houston

Dallas

Phoenix–Mesa

Orange County, Cal.

Washington, D.C. metropolitan area

Seattle–Belleview– Everett

Los Angeles–Long Beach

San Diego

Tampa–St. Petersburg– Clearwater

Chicago

Minneapolis–St. Paul

Denver

Riverside–San Bernadino

Orlando

Portland, Ore.– Vancouver, Wash.

Sacramento

Las Vegas

Austin–San Marcos

San Jose

Source: National Planning Association

WHERE TO LOOK

No matter how qualified you are, a job opening must exist to make a match. Metropolitan areas in the U.S. that lead in job opportunities are published annually in various periodicals. As with job growth in smaller companies, the most rapid geographical job growth is in areas with less than 500,000 in population. In other words, there is a downsizing in location as well as corporate structure. Consider, too:

1. **Smaller growing companies** are located throughout the country and especially in states with business-friendly environments, such as Washington, Oregon, the Carolinas, Utah and Tennessee.

2. **University towns** offer opportunity for those who like the college connection. States such as Nebraska, Indiana, Virginia and the Carolinas have universities that are acting as incubators, which provide start-up space, advice and support for new businesses.

3. **Growing retirement areas**—such as Florida, Arizona, Arkansas, Nevada, New Mexico, South Carolina and Texas—provide great opportunities in agencies and businesses providing services to the elderly.

4. **Resort areas,** such as Colorado, Tennessee, Florida and Texas, offer jobs as well as fun.

5. **Sleepers,** including states such as Idaho, Iowa, Missouri and the Dakotas, where businesses are growing because of the lower cost of living and doing business.

6. **Big cities,** including Boston, Los Angeles, Chicago and New York, where big businesses are again hiring because of increased company profits.

Suggested Reading

- *Where the Jobs Are*
  Joyce Hadley, Career Press

THE INTERNATIONAL SCENE

Today's economic headlines signaling a "global economy" have created visions of working-vacation opportunities. The reality is that there is no such thing as a global job market. So before you start to conduct a global job search, consider the following:

- **Local nationals** tend to get hired before foreigners.

- **It is less expensive** for a company to hire locally.

- **To compete against local nationals,** you must have a unique skill they don't have.

- **Even if you have the technical expertise,** language skills and legal approvals, you may not have the knowledge and sensitivity to establish effective working relationships in a culture you didn't grow up in.

If your romantic visions are now more tempered and you are still interested in the international field, what should you do? Your best bet is to work in the U.S. for a firm operating overseas. Get to know the basics and develop the necessary skills and then you can move abroad. Think globally for the long-term, but look locally now.

Suggested Reading

If you are determined to work overseas now, here are some resources you may wish to use in your campaign:

- *The Complete Guide to International Jobs & Careers*
  Ronald and Caryl Krannich, Impact Publications

- *How to Get a Job in Europe*
  Robert Sanborn, Surrey Books

- *International Jobs*
  Eric Kocher, Addison Wesley

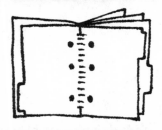

PART

THREE

Plan Your Job Campaign

TURN WISHES INTO ACTION

By now you should be aware of your career values, interests and skills. Also, you should be able to link these issues to the current workplace. The next step is to plan your personal job campaign. The major elements of any job campaign are:

- **Establishing** your career goals.

- **Planning** your job campaign.

- **Organizing** your job campaign.

- **Preparing** marketing materials.

- **Carrying out** job campaign tactics.

- **Obtaining** feedback, evaluating results and making adjustments.

All of the elements are discussed in this book. Once you're familiar with them, you'll be ready to prepare your job campaign plan.

A plan will make your job search easier, less frustrating and more successful. Visualize what you want to be, then translate that vision into a job campaign goal. Determine a strategy to reach your goal. Next, list the major steps necessary to implement that strategy. Finally, target and contact the key people who can help you. (See the sample Job Campaign Plan on page 36.)

Remember, everyone works with a different timetable. The trick is to find what works for you and stick with it. If you can afford to take the summer off after graduation, relax and enjoy yourself—you will probably spend the rest of your life working. If you don't have that luxury, you'll want to begin your job campaign well before graduation.

Dick Clark, television personality and producer, earned his bachelor's degree in advertising from Syracuse University.

Kevin Costner, actor, film producer and director, earned a bachelor's degree in marketing at Cal State, Fullerton.

Martha Stewart, diva of home arts and entertaining, once was a stockbroker on Wall Street.

Gail Sheehy, author of Passages and other books about life changes, began her working life as a traveling home economist for J.C. Penney.

HOW TO USE YOUR JOB CAMPAIGN PLAN

Use your Job Campaign Plan to get started in the right direction and to keep moving ahead on target. Your plan contains your job goal, your job campaign strategy to achieve that goal, key steps to carry out your strategy, and the names of people you need to contact to make things happen. Because planning is a process, your plan should be updated weekly. The elements of your plan are:

Job goal

State what you want to be, with what type of organization and what skills you bring to the job. You may restate this goal in your résumé. (See page 74.)

Job-search strategy

What is your overall approach to achieve your goal? What resources will you utilize? (See page 46.)

Major tasks to carry out strategy

What are the important tasks you need to perform to carry out your job campaign strategy? (See Parts Four, Five and Six.)

Key people to contact

Nothing happens until you start talking with people. Who are the people you need to talk with to develop your network of contacts? (See page 65.)

Comments

Write down any details you may want to refer to later that have not been listed above.

You should not finalize your job campaign plan until you are familiar with all the parts of this book. However, it is never too early to start thinking about the critical elements of your plan and to make notes for future reference. Review the following sample Job Campaign Plan.

Sample Job Campaign Plan

Job Goal
Obtain a position as a writer with a public relations firm utilizing my degree in English, my word processing and desktop publishing skills, and my staff writing experience

Job-Search Strategy
Develop a network of contacts using the Public Relations Society of America (PRSA) and members of my personal network

Major Tasks to Carry Out Strategy
1. *Contact PRSA to obtain Washington, DC, membership list and information packet*
2. *Write résumé and cover letter*
3. *Target individuals for information interviews*
4. *Script telephone approach*
5. *Prepare list of questions for information interview*

Key People to Contact
1. *Director of Communications—Public Relations Society of America*
2. *Friend who works for American Society of Association Executives*
3. *Friend who is staff aide for U.S. Congressman*
4. *Friend at travel agency who uses public relations firm*
5. *Brother's friend who is building manager with public relations firm tenant*
6. *College business communications instructor*
7. *Friend of friend who works as reporter for the Washington Post*
8. *Friend of parents who is manager of an advertising firm*
9. *Friend of friend who works for personnel search firm*
10. *Friend of friend who works for government contractor doing environmental clean-up*

Comments
Organize work space
Give parents job-search progress report
Sign up for online service's free trial offer

Job Campaign Plan

Job Goal

_____

_____

Job-Search Strategy

_____

_____

Major Tasks to Carry Out Strategy

1. _____
2. _____
3. _____
4. _____
5. _____

Key People to Contact

1. _____
2. _____
3. _____
4. _____
5. _____
6. _____
7. _____
8. _____
9. _____
10. _____

Comments

_____

_____

_____

_____

SURVIVE WHILE YOU CAMPAIGN

Too bad academe never offered courses on cash flow, expense budgeting or credit management. The economic realities of living on your own, especially while you're trying to launch your career, can be overwhelming. Food, rent, clothing, transportation and school loans all seem to hit at once. Then your parents explain that you now have to obtain your own health insurance, car insurance and phone credit card. The lure of instant money via credit cards is a trap awaiting many unsuspecting big spenders. Numerous small purchases add up faster than you realize. All these expenses and no income. It doesn't seem fair. What do you do? Here are some tips:

Shelter

- **If you are job-searching near your parents' home,** ask to live with them during your search. Establish a written agreement with your parents regarding monthly payments, terms and conditions, such as duration, as well as rights and responsibilities of both parties. This helps establish a mutual understanding that can make life easier for everyone.

- **Because you may lack steady income,** you may wish to establish a barter system with your parents. For example, in exchange for room and board, you can wash cars, cut grass, pick up groceries, cook some meals and take out the trash.

George P. Radanovich, U.S. representative from California, holds a degree in business agriculture and was a vintner before being elected to public office.

Patty Murray, U.S. senator from Washington, earned her degree in recreational therapy.

Most Popular Majors

The six most popular undergraduate majors at four-year colleges in 1996 were, in this order:

Business
Psychology
Education
Elementary education
Nursing
Biological sciences

- **Accept it: Although you have been semi-independent for the past few years,** it is difficult for your parents to stop trying to take care of you after twenty-plus years, especially if you are living at home. Also, do household chores without being asked. Practice the kind of initiative you'll want to show at your new job.

- **If family or friends do not have room for you,** check the classified ads for house-sitting opportunities or for room rentals in private homes.

- **If you are job-searching away from home,** try to find temporary shelter with people who travel much of the time, such as auditors, flight attendants, or people who work different shifts, such as nurses or law enforcement officers. Establish an agreement to pay a portion of the rent week to week or month to month. Do not sign a lease unless it is month to month only.

Health Insurance

- **Coverage under your parents' policy** usually ends when you stop being a full-time student or when you reach age 23 or 25, depending on the policy. Once you have a job, you may be able to join the employer-sponsored group coverage.

- **Insurers offer short-term policies** (three, six or twelve months) at reasonable cost. Such policies may be renewable, typically for up to a year. Also, any major illness during this time may be excluded from coverage on a future policy due to a common clause concerning pre-existing conditions.

Transportation

- **Don't buy a car until you have a job.** Even then, wait until you have your expenses under control. Ask about discounts for recent college graduates.

- **A car means extra costs** for insurance, taxes and maintenance.

- **A nearly new car** (less than a year old) can cost thousands less than a new car.

- **Many larger cities** have companies that rent used cars for a short while, like a week or month.

- **Walk, ride your bike** or use public transportation when possible.

Credit Cards

- **Limit yourself to one** general-purpose credit card that has no annual fee.

- **Maintain a balance of less than** $500 or 50% of what you have in a savings account. Make your monthly payments on time.

- **Special-purpose credit cards,** such as telephone and gasoline cards, are for convenience—not borrowing. Pay them in full each month.

Clothing

- **Maintain a basic interview wardrobe** that's always clean and pressed.

- **Don't buy any clothing that is not discounted** at least 20%—otherwise you've paid too much.

Money

- **Develop a monthly budget**—including savings—and stick to it.

- **Maintain at least $1,000** in your savings account for emergencies.

Most Job Offers

In 1996, students receiving the most job offers were those who earned bachelor's degrees in:

Accounting
Mechanical engineering
Economics and finance

- **You are starting to establish a credit history** that is important to your career. Many companies conduct credit checks as part of a complete background investigation prior to issuing a job offer.

Taxes

- **As a first-time job holder, it's likely you will be taking the standard deduction** rather than itemizing. Regardless, job-search expenses for your first job are not deductible. After that, expenses must exceed 2% of your adjusted gross income, and you must be searching for a job in the same line of work.

- **If you expect to work continuously for no more than about eight months** during the year, ask your employer to use a special part-year method to compute your withholding for taxes. This method is based on actual earnings, versus a full year's earnings, and will provide more take-home pay.

Monthly Cash Flow Worksheet

If you haven't already begun to track your income and expenses, it's a great habit to develop, even if you aren't currently receiving a regular paycheck.

Reproduce one copy of the worksheet for each month of the year. That will allow you to account for items that may change from month to month. File your worksheets in a separate section at the back of your job-search organizing notebook.

If you need to cut back, focus first on expenses unrelated to survival and a successful job search. Remember, living cheaply can mean greater independence and adventure. It could even become a way of life.

Month _____

Income

Wages, salary, tips
    (after taxes) $ _____
Loans   _____
Gifts   _____
Total Income $ _____

Expenses

Job search (inc. supplies,
    printing, postage,
    telephone, online time,
    special travel)   _____
Rent (or mortgage)   _____
Food (groceries)   _____
Utilities (inc. electricity,
    gas, oil, water/sewer,
    garbage, telephone)   _____
Savings (for emergencies,
    investments, vacations,
    other)   _____
Public transportation
    (inc. parking)   _____
Auto loan   _____
Auto insurance   _____
Misc. auto expenses (gas, oil,
    repairs, fees and taxes)   _____

Health insurance   _____
Medical, dental and
    eye-care bills not
    covered by insurance   _____
Credit card payments   _____
Loan payments   _____
Clothing (inc. dry
    cleaning, laundry)   _____
Personal care (inc. hair cuts)   _____
Home maintenance
    (inc. furnishings, paint)   _____
Educational expenses   _____
Recreation/entertainment
    (inc. eating out, movies,
    clubs, cable TV, CDs,
    books, gym membership)   _____
Vacations   _____
Gifts   _____
Total Expenses $ _____

Total Income $ _____
Total Expenses   − _____
Net Cash Flow,
or Discretionary Income $ _____

ORGANIZE YOUR JOB CAMPAIGN

GET IT TOGETHER

This book will help you get organized by teaching you to arrange your job campaign activities into manageable tasks and schedule activities in the right order for maximum productivity. You'll also want to:

- **Keep all critical information** regarding your job campaign in your own job-search organizing notebook for convenience and effective follow-up.

- **Dedicate a specific location** in your home to your job campaign. Ideally, it should contain a desk or table, chair, lamp, telephone, filing box with folders and large wastebasket.

- **Buy an answering machine** or telephone-service option to receive return calls while you are out.

- **Create a computer directory and files** for your job search. This will help you find information quickly during a phone call. If you prefer, you can create or recreate your notebook on your computer.

- **Choose a calendar**—a very personal decision. Monthly calendars provide the long-term picture. Weekly calendars provide a more manageable timetable and daily calendars provide a specific schedule of tasks to be accomplished that day.

Good things happen when you're organized. It's that simple.

HOW TO USE YOUR DAILY JOB CAMPAIGN CALENDAR

The key to success is to use the type of calendar with which you are most comfortable. Usually a combination works best for most of us in most situations. However, in a job campaign, you need a calendar that produces results. The Daily Job Campaign Calendar is designed to help you make things happen every day. To get maximum benefit from it:

- **First, prepare three to five daily calendars** with items from your Job Campaign Plan (see Part Three).

- **On each day,** fill in future calendars as you progress. For example, if a contact says, "call me back in three weeks," start your calendar for that day with that instruction for yourself.

- **As each item is completed,** check it off.

- **At the end of each day,** evaluate your progress and complete your calendar for the next day.

- **When you obtain a referral or complete an appointment,** write your follow-up actions on your calendar.

- **For convenience and effective follow-up,** reproduce your Daily Job Campaign Calendar forms and place them in your job-search organizing notebook.

Daily Job Campaign Calendar

Date _____ *Day of Week* _____

Appointments and Interviews (Enter into Networking Directory, Action Log and Job Prospect Profile; see pages 71, 89 and 106–107.)

Name	*Location*	*Time*

Phone Calls (Enter into appropriate form, see above.)

Name	*Telephone Number*

New Referrals (Enter into Networking Directory.)

Name	*Telephone Number*

Résumés to Mail (Enter into Action Log.)

Name	*Organization*

Follow-Up Letters and Thank-You Notes to Mail
(Enter into Networking Directory or Action Log.)

Name	*Organization*

First lady Hillary Rodham Clinton earned her undergraduate degree in political science from Wellesley College and her law degree from Yale.

ORGANIZE YOUR INFORMATION SOURCES

In this information age, the key issues in a job campaign are:

- What do I need?
- Where is it available?
- How do I use it?

The remainder of Part Four answers these questions and shows you how to get the information you need promptly, efficiently and inexpensively. We focus on six sources of job campaign information:

- Campus career services
- The public library
- Online services
- Trade and professional associations
- Personnel search firms
- Your personal network

CAMPUS CAREER SERVICES
(An Often Overlooked Resource)

Most colleges and universities offer a wide range of career- and job-search services to develop career-planning skills, teach job-search techniques and arrange contacts between students and employees. Typically, these services include:

Career resource library

Information including career guides, job descriptions, salary surveys, videotapes, employer information, and electronic information services are available in most centers.

Job listings

Information about full-time or part-time jobs, summer jobs and internships may be available in print, or via computer or touch-tone-telephone access.

Workshops

Some campuses have regularly scheduled career planning and job-search workshops.

Consulting services

Career consultants may be available to discuss career- and job-search issues. They may include services such as critiques of résumés and evaluations of videotaped practice interviews.

Clint Eastwood, actor, film producer and director, dropped out of the business administration program at Los Angeles College.

The Public Library (A Gold Mine)

The public library is one of the most underrated resources for job-hunting. It is a gold mine of information. The following list is just a sample of what is available. Spend a day at the library exploring; the more you do, the more information you will turn up. It doesn't hurt to make the reference librarian your best friend; he or she can uncover valuable resources and leads you may not find on your own.

Surveying the field
- *American Almanac of Jobs & Salaries*
- *Current Job Listings*
- *Dictionary of Occupational Titles*
- *Occupational Outlook Handbook*
- *U.S. Industrial Outlook*

State and county
- *MacRae's State Industrial Directory*
- State industrial directory
- County directory of business
- Local chamber of commerce directory
- Interstate job bank
- Statewide job opportunities
- County job list

Large companies
- *Dun & Bradstreet Million Dollar Directory*
- *Hoover's Employer Directories*
- *Moody's Industrial Manual*
- *Standard & Poor's Register of Corporations*
- *Value Line Investment Survey*

Federal government
- *171 Reference Book (Government Job Application)*
- *Federal Career Opportunities*
- *How to Get a Federal Job*
- *U.S. Government Manual*

International
- *The Almanac of International Jobs and Careers*
- *The Complete Guide to International Jobs*
- *Directory of Overseas Summer Jobs*
- *European Markets*
- *Guide to Careers in World Affairs*
- *How to Get a Job in Europe*
- *International Careers*

Specialty publications
- Association directories
- *Business to Business Yellow Pages*
- *Directory of Directories*
- *Directory of Executive Recruiters*
- *Peterson's Guides*
- *Worldwide Chamber of Commerce Directory*

Newsletters
- *Career Opportunities News*
- *Career Waves*
- *Kennedy's Career Strategist*

Periodicals
- *ASAE (American Society of Association Executives) Career Opps*
- *Environmental Career Opportunities*
- *International Career Employment Opportunities*
- *National AdSearch*
- *National and Federal Legal Employment Report*
- *National Business Employment Weekly*
- *Opportunities in Public Affairs*

Job fairs

Employers representing various organizations set up booths in one location to talk personally about job prospects. Many job fairs are sponsored by consortia of colleges or professional organizations.

Campus interviews

Employers visit the campus each year to conduct preliminary interviews. This is a great way to gain interview experience, get plugged into the recruiting process, and maybe even get a job.

Alumni office

Many alumni offices offer referral services or lists of alumni whom you might contact. Check the Alumni Directory for possible networking contacts in your location of choice.

Job-Hunting Online
(Get Wired, Get Hired)

You've heard about and likely experienced all the fun stuff you can do when you connect up with an online service or jump onto the Internet—like playing games or meeting people from all over the nation or even the world in chat rooms or newsgroups to talk about your favorite subjects. But now you might want to chase your dream job. In brief, here's what you can do online:

- **post** your résumé,

- **scan** electronic classified ads,

- **research** corporate information, and

- **network** electronically.

Odds Are

Three-fourths of the college graduates who enter the labor force between 1994 and 2005 can expect to find jobs requiring college degrees.

Michael Dell, founder of Dell Computers, Inc., dropped out of pre-med at the University of Texas at the end of his freshman year.

William Gates, co-founder and CEO of Microsoft, dropped out of pre-law at Harvard at the end of his sophomore year.

Each of these functions is discussed later in this section. However, here are some general guidelines:

- **The more technical the job you're looking for, the more likely your success.** A Java programmer will land a job online faster than an English major, unless the English major wants to edit Web pages. That's because technical skills are easily quantifiable and qualifications are easily specified with key words.

- **The online world facilitates quick exchange of communications, information and knowledge.** You can present yourself however you like. But landing a job still requires a face-to-face interview, and once hired, you must deal with real people in your daily work life.

- **Be careful out there.** In cyberspace you become potentially known by millions of people who can contact you in a heartbeat. Not all of them are harmless, and most often you won't really know who you're dealing with. The best practice: Use a post office box address, a telephone answering machine and possibly an "alias" online until you can verify that your correspondents are who and what they claim to be.

The Internet

The Internet, the infamous "information superhighway," is the computer network of networks linking millions of computers world-wide. You can use the Internet to send electronic mail, access databases, retrieve files, carry on conversations and participate in discussions, in text, on a variety of subjects. You'll find much of the job-search information you want on the World Wide Web, the Internet's commercial network.

Chances are, you already know that because you've been using the Internet at school. You may even have had free access via a student account. But once you graduate, there's no more free ride. You'll have to buy access on your own (unless your parents already have a service provider and will foot the bill for your online time). If you don't have a computer at home, check in with public or university libraries in your area to see if they have public terminals that you can pay to use.

Getting Ready to Go Online

- **You'll need to hook up with an Internet service provider (ISP),** such as AT&T, MCI, Sprint or a regional provider, to access the Internet directly, or

- **Use an online service** (see page 54), if you want the additional features that they offer.

- **Check out the various pricing structures,** whether a flat monthly fee or a charge for time spent online, and take advantage of any free test drives.

- **To access the Web, you'll need a Web browser,** such as *Netscape Navigator (http://www.netscape.com)* or *Microsoft Internet Explorer (http://www.microsoft. com/ie/ie.html)* . You can download a free copy of these programs to start, but you'll eventually have to pay for updates.

- **If you are not computer savvy,** find a qualified friend or acquaintance who is willing to be your technical mentor, or check out the resources listed below. It will save you time, money and sanity.

A Few Pointers on Using the Web

- **Try the various search engines,** such as Alta Vista and Yahoo (see the accompanying list), to locate information and Web sites. Each search engine will produce differing outcomes given the same search string (the key word or words you're searching with).

- **Or, jump directly to the many job-related resources listed in this chapter by using their URLs** (Uniform Resource Locator), which are like phone numbers.

Search Engines

Alta Vista
http://altavista.digital.com

Infoseek
http://guide.infoseek.com

Lycos
http://www.lycos.com

Web Crawler
http://www.webcrawler. com

Yahoo
http://www.yahoo.com

(See also Starting Point, page 58.)

Internet Questions Answered Online

World Wide Web FAQ
*http://www.boutell.com/
faq*

**The World Wide Web
Primer**
*http://www.vuw.ac.nz/
~gnat/ideas/www-
primer.html*

- **Don't give up if your early attempts lead to inappropriate sites or data.** Just be more specific as you go.

- **When you find a likely Web site,** explore it fully by using the hypertext links provided.

- **Many Web sites also provide hypertext links to other related or recommended Web sites,** so you can get from here to there instantly (well almost). For example, a "position available" listing in a job bank may be linked directly to the company listing the opening.

- **You'll feel like you've won the lottery if** you find a Web site that features hypertext bibliographies and reference lists. This is typical of Web sites created by trade associations and nonprofit and professional organizations. Just keep following the leads.

- **Stay focused.** The Web is a place to explore, try different options and learn by trial and error. But remember to stick to your job search. Avoid spending valuable time on interesting, but irrelevant material. You might even set an online time limit for yourself. For example, you could reserve an hour at the end of the day—after you've made all your phone calls and implemented the rest of your job-hunting plan for that day.

Online Job-Hunting Mentors

For specific online job-hunting advice and leads, here are three resources developed by people who have experience you can draw from. These resources are updated regularly and the references are pre-screened.

- **College Grad Job Hunter**
  http://www.collegegrad.com

- **Dr. Dane Spearing's Job Hunt Page**
  http://www.job-hunt.org

- **Margaret F. Riley's Internet Job Guide**
  http://www.jobtrak.com/jobguide

Five Hot Web Sites for New Grads

- **Cool Works**
  http://www.coolworks.com/showme
  Includes seasonal job listings for ski resorts, cruise lines and national parks.

- **Job Direct**
  http://www.jobdirect.com
  Matches companies looking for soon-to-graduate students with applicants.

- **JobTrak**
  http://www.jobtrack.com
  Features more than 2,000 new job listings per day, but it's restricted to current students and alumni of universities. You need to get your school's password from its career center.

- **JobWeb**
  http://www.jobweb.org
  Maintained by the National Association of Colleges and Employers with thousands of postings and more than 50 links to career information.

- **Monster Board**
  http://www.monster.com
  Search U.S. and international job listings by location and discipline. "Jobba-the-Hunt" acts as your personal job-search agent; you log in, and it hunts for appropriate job listings 24 hours a day.

Suggested Reading

- *Be Your Own Headhunter Online*
  Pam Dixon and Sylvia Tiersten, Random House

Phil Jackson, coach of the Chicago Bulls basketball team, majored in philosophy, psychology and religion at the University of North Dakota and originally wanted a career in the ministry.

- *Hook Up, Get Hired!*
  Joyce Lain Kennedy, John Wiley & Sons, Inc.

- *The Internet Starter Kit for the Mac*
  Adam C. Engst, Hayden Books

- *On Line Job Search Companion*
  James C. Gonyea, McGraw-Hill

- *The Online User's Encyclopedia*
  Bernard Aboba, Addison-Wesley Publishing Co.

- *The Whole Internet User's Guide and Catalog*
  Ed Krol, O'Reilly & Associates

Online Services to Choose From

Besides their job-search-related content, each of these services also allows you to access the Internet.

- **America Online**
  800–827–6364; *http://www.aol.com*
  AOL wants to be known as the full-service job source and goes a long way toward its goal. Besides providing a place to post your résumé and talk jobs with others, AOL's Career Center offers an array of services, including career counseling and a series of career-analysis exercises you can download to your computer. When you're online with AOL, type the keyword career to reach the Career Center.

- **CompuServe**
  800–848–8199; *http://www.compuserve.com*
  CompuServe offers Sprynet, an Internet service provider and CompuServe Interactive (CSi), its traditional offering with classified ads and special interest forums. Hundreds of jobs are posted among the electronic classified ads on CSi. Beware, though, of options in the employment-and-education category with such come-ons as "EARN TOP PAY! WORK AT HOME!" and "EASY MONEY!" Many are of question-

able value to most people. For electronic networking, the forums provide a convenient and efficient means to target an audience. You can also reach E-Span here.

- **Prodigy**
  800–776–3449; *http://www.prodigy.com*
  Prodigy Classic, the original Prodigy, won't allow you to post your résumé in its system, but you can share referrals and information about jobs with fellow Prodigy members. Prodigy Internet (PI) uses Microsoft's Internet Explorer as its default Web browser. Chat, e-mail, Internet newsgroups, and Prodigy content are integrated.

Playing the Electronic Résumé Lottery

Résumé databases typically contain thousands of résumés or profiles catalogued by key words (buzzwords) reflecting industry, location, skills, education and experience. Employers can scan the résumés for job candidates on demand, 24 hours a day, seven days a week and contact them directly via telephone or e-mail. To ensure that they're providing employers with "active" candidates, the services may delete résumés after they've been posted for three to six months.

The advantage of these services to you is the exposure you get. In many cases you don't even need a computer to use them. The disadvantage for first-time job seekers is the lack of a work history for your profile. But skills are skills, and if you have them, flaunt them.

Here are some of the résumé data banks:

- **Cors**
  800–323–1352
  Cors maintains a data bank of what it estimates is 1.5 million names, supplied by job seekers, employers eliminating or downsizing positions, and universities. The processing fee is $25. Your résumé stays in the system indefinitely (which may account for the size of the data base). You can update whenever you like for free.

Raymond Flynn, U.S. Ambassador to the Vatican and former mayor of Boston, attended Providence College on a basketball scholarship and was drafted by the Syracuse Nationals (now the Philadelphia 76ers).

Matt Groening, creator of The Simpsons, *graduated from Evergreen State College, which offers no majors. One of his first jobs was ghostwriting the autobiography of an elderly film director who also employed him as his chauffeur.*

- **DORS**
  800–727–3677; *telnet://TBB.DM.DC.OSD.MIL*
  The Defense Outplacement Referral System is a free service for military personnel and their spouses about to leave active duty. DORS keeps more than 21,000 résumés online for up to 180 days.

- **National Résumé Bank**
  3637 Fourth St. North, Suite 330, St. Petersburg, FL 33704; 813–896–3694
  One of the most job-hunter-friendly of the data-base services, NRB keeps you notified with monthly updates on how many companies have reviewed the summary of your qualifications that it keys into its 2,500-résumé data base. When a company asks for a copy of your résumé, you get a card in the mail. Sponsored by the Professional Association of Résumé Writers, the service sorts candidates into 35 job categories, such as engineering and health care. To sign up, send $40 and five copies of your résumé to the above address. After that, you're in the system for as long as you want.

- **Online Career Center**
  317–293–6499; *http://www.occ.com*
  Online's data base isn't skewed toward technical jobs. It contains some 20,000 résumés and it's growing. You can leave your résumé at the Internet address occ-resumes@occ.com, or you can send your résumé and a check for $10 to Online Résumé Service, 2780 Waterfront Parkway, Suite 100, Indianapolis, IN 46214). Online will key it in for you. Your listing will stay in the system for three months (six months if you paid the $10 fee by mail). Then if you haven't updated your résumé, your records are purged. The service also solicits help-wanted listings from employers, usually posting between 16,000 and 18,000 job vacancies.

- **SkillSearch**
  800–252–5665; *http://www.internet-is.com/skillsearch*

If you belong to one of the more than 125 sponsoring college alumni associations nationwide—including public and private schools—that are members of SkillSearch, you can take advantage of your alma mater's good name and network with your fellow alumni. But you don't have to be an alumnus to use SkillSearch's services. The SkillSearch electronic data base contains more than 65,000 résumés. Enrollment is $65 for the first year and $15 per year after that. Résumé updates are free and encouraged.

Cruising the Electronic Classifieds

To obtain faster responses, many employers are using electronic classified ads. Specialized vendors distribute their paid job advertisements to multiple online services. You can search many of the online services' (see pages 54–55) bulletin boards for job-listing databases and other employment-related information. If you want to chase classifieds, some of the big players are:

- **Career Connections**
  415–903–5800; *http://www.career.com*
  The service is free to job hunters; look for a section devoted to listings for new graduates. High-tech companies such as IBM, Texas Instruments and Okidata use Career Connections to post openings.

- **E-Span**
  800–682–2901; *http://www.espan.com*
  E-Span's 3,000 to 4,000 job openings are updated twice weekly. Listings are paid for by employers, so there's no charge to you. You can also get to E-Span via CompuServe (go word e-span) or find it in the misc.jobs.offered Internet newsgroup.

- **Federal Job Opportunity Board**
  912–757–3030
  Its menu-driven program is easy to use. Connect by computer at 912–757–3100. Job openings in the federal government are updated nightly. The service is

Online Classifieds

Search for your dream job by location and job category. Many of these Web sites allow you to post your résumé, too.

America's Job Bank
http://www.ajb.dni.us
Provides links to Web sites of state employment services so you can check state job banks.

Career Magazine
http://www.careermag.com
Daily download of job listings from major Internet job newsgroups.

Career Mosaic
http://www.careermosaic.com
Employer profiles and job listings.

Career Path
http://www.careerpath.com
Daily updates of job listings by contributing newspapers, including the Chicago Tribune, L.A. Times, and N.Y. Times.

Good Works
http://www.essential.org/goodworks
Public-interest jobs.

Singer Paula Abdul was studying sports broadcasting at California State University when she dropped out during her sophomore year to become one of the Laker Girls.

free except for your long-distance phone charge. If you live in a large city, you can get job information for your area by calling the regional Office of Personnel Management for a local access number.

Browsing Virtual Offices

Thousands of businesses and other organizations have Web sites, enabling you to, in effect, visit corporate sites without ever leaving home. Also, many companies are now placing "position available" announcements on their Web sites.

Keep in mind that your success in landing your dream job depends in part on how well you do your homework. With the Web, your easy access to career information and job leads is virtually unlimited except by your willingness to work at it. Go for it!

A starting point

How do you find these companies? One way is via a Web site called "Starting Point" *(http://www.stpt.com)*. You can type in a company name or job-specific area of interest, select a search engine of choice from the menu, and you'll get a list of hypertext referrals to related Web sites.

To find out about about publicly owned companies

- **The SEC** (*http://www.sec.gov;* select the Edgar Database of Corporate Information). If you find a job opportunity with a publicly owned company (meaning its shares of stock are publicly tracked on a stock exchange), you can go directly to the U.S. Securities and Exchange Commission for legal information and financial data the company is required to file. One of the best bets for current data is a company's Form 10-K, basically an annual report without the usual hype.

- **Business directories.** If you subscribe to an online service, you can check to see if directories, indexes or other sources are available. Or, if you have access to the Web, you can use "starting point" (see above) and type in the key words "corporate directories" to get you started." Check for any of the resources listed on page 48 to see if they're available online yet.

Privately owned companies

Information regarding privately owned companies, subsidiaries of large corporations, small local firms and foreign-owned companies is more difficult to find. In these cases, local chambers of commerce, trade associations or public libraries are your best bet, and as more and more people use the Web, these organizations will develop Web pages to meet the demands of their following.

Create Your Own Web Page

A potentially powerful way to promote yourself on the Web is to create your Web page using graphics, pictures, sound effects and video clips to offer an exciting multimedia presentation of your skills.

Most of the online services let you set up a Web page with on-screen, fill-in-the-blank forms. The result is an acceptable online billboard.

Also, there are sites to visit on the Internet that offer advice and counsel for good Web page design (see the box on the following page).

Bryant Gumbel, broadcast journalist, was a sales representative for a paper bag and folding carton manufacturer.

If you are clueless or you really want to get serious about promoting yourself, consider trying and buying *My Internet Business Page* (800–325–3508; *http://www.mysoftware.com*). The software provides an array of predesigned templates, headlines and artwork for laying out your Web page.

Give some thought to what you want to put on your page. Possibilities include your portrait and biographical sketch, samples of your work (say, writing or graphic design). To see what others are doing, visit Cool Site of the Day *(http://cool.infi.net)* and the Useless Page *(http://www.go2net.com/internet/useless)*.

When you are ready for your world debut, let the public know where to find it by announcing your page via Submit It, a Web feature that you can reach at *http://www.submit–it.com.*

Now, as a Web Master, you are ready for all the world to come visit your home page. Brace yourself for some interesting experiences and wild times.

TRADE AND PROFESSIONAL ASSOCIATIONS
(A Trade Secret)

More than 50% of all new jobs come from the more than 13,500,000 small businesses in the U.S. Many of these small businesses belong to trade and professional associations. There now exists an association for practically every type of business or industry. It makes sense, then, that associations are an ideal source of information and contacts regarding the industry, companies and people they represent.

Trade associations are non-profit, cooperative, voluntary organizations of competitors in the same industry. They combine financial and human resources to deal with mutual business interests and problems, such as government regulations, industry statistics, standardization, international trade, and legal and accounting issues. An association may have a staff of one person or hundreds of people.

Almost all associations maintain a membership directory. These directories are often available free or for a minimal price. In addition, they may also publish newsletters, books, magazines, surveys and reports that will help you do your homework on a company or an industry.

One problem facing most growing industries today is a shortage of knowledgeable people. For them, career development is a high priority. Many of these associations provide catalogs or listings of career materials and programs. Catalogs may include recruitment brochures, scholarship pamphlets, industry reports, education programs, tapes, films and videos, and career placement information.

Some associations also operate a job referral service. The service may consist of newsletter listings, a computer database or a formal referral service. Even if a referral service does not exist, the trade association personnel can be a valuable network resource. They can be very effective in directing you to the right people and places.

When calling an association, ask whether it has an employment referral service or career resource center. This may take persistence. Make sure you speak to a staff person who can help you get the information you want and be sure to explain exactly who you are and why you're calling. Ask for membership directories, education and training materials, special reports and referrals to specific leaders in your geographic area.

Association Directories

Association directories may be found in most libraries. They provide association names, addresses and phone numbers, membership information and descriptions of associations' missions. The following association directories collectively offer more than 10,500 listings representing 287 million members:

Association Jobs

For a weekly online listing of entry-level job opportunities with nonprofit organizations, check out ASAE Career Starters. It's featured on the Web site of the American Society of Association Executives. You'll find it at:

http://www.asaenet.org/ aboutasae/jobservices/ cstarter.html

While in law school at the University of Alabama, Millard Fuller, founder of Habitat for Humanity, and Morris S. Dees, Jr., co-founder of the Southern Poverty Law Conference, invested in real estate. They renovated the properties themselves and rented them out to students.

- *Ayer's Association Directory*

- *Gale Global Access: Encyclopedia of Associations*

- *National Trade and Professional Associations*

PERSONNEL SEARCH FIRMS
(What They Can and Cannot Do for You)

Firms that assist employers in finding job candidates are referred to by many names, such as search firms, personnel consultants, executive recruiters, employment agencies or headhunters. They come in two varieties: those whose fees are paid by employers and those whose fees are paid by job candidates.

Fees Paid By Company

- **Retained search.** The search firm is retained on an exclusive basis, and the fee is paid regardless of the results of the search. Typically, this approach is for executive-level talent, not recent graduates.

- **Contingency search.** The fee is paid only if the candidate referred by the search firm is hired. This speculative approach may be appropriate for graduates with specific skills in demand by the workplace. The newly hired person may have to promise to stay with the firm at least six months. If he or she doesn't stay, the search firm must reimburse the employer a prorated portion of the fee. Sometimes the employer will try to recover the cost from the employee.

Fees Paid By Job Candidate

- **Contingency placement.** The candidate pays the fee only if he or she accepts the position. Many times, a contingency firm hunts for résumés to broadcast locally. Most firms hiring young professionals would rather hire directly than pay a fee to contingency recruiters. Beware of high pressure tactics used to get you to take a job that may not be what you want. Read the fine print and never prepay any fee.

- **Employment services.** Career evaluations, résumé preparation and practice interviewing services are offered to job candidates for a fee. Always ask for references, work samples and the opportunity to meet the person who will work on your behalf.

You must be extremely careful to use only highly reputable contingency firms. Ask for references and check each one out. Does the search firm belong to a professional association? Is it certified? Some less-professional firms may, in addition to pressuring you to take a job you don't want, present your credentials to many companies indiscriminately in order to obtain a fee. On the other hand, there are many reputable agencies with established company relationships and valuable industry contacts. Use professional and trade associations to find those agencies that may increase your chances of getting the right job. They may also give you helpful counseling, interview tips, career ideas and résumé help.

A Final Word

Always call a search firm prior to writing a letter. Most letters from inexperienced candidates are ignored. Handle the call similarly to a call for any information interview (see page 66). If you are asked to send a résumé, make sure your cover letter is addressed to the person with whom you spoke. Always follow up to make sure the person has received it and to determine the next step.

Amy Tan, author of The Joy Luck Club and other books, holds bachelor's and master's degrees in linguistics. Her first job: She was a development consultant to the Alameda County Association for Retarded Citizens.

After high school, Carroll Shelby, designer of the Ford Cobra and co-designer of the Dodge Viper, rode his motorcycle as a mail dispatcher.

Suggested Reading

- *The Directory of Executive Recruiters*
  Kennedy Publications, Fitzwilliam, NH
  603–585–6544

YOUR PROFESSIONAL NETWORK

("Know Who" Versus "Know How")

Networking is the cultivation and use of personal contacts to exchange information and obtain additional referrals. In a job campaign you need information regarding careers, companies, jobs and people. The best sources for this information are personal contacts.

Why Use Networking?

- **Between 60% and 70% of all jobs are filled** through networking.

- **One-on-one contact is the most effective way** to get yourself hired.

- **You can learn about unpublished job requirements** before your competition does.

- **You gain a competitive edge** by being referred directly to a potential employer rather than by being processed through a recruiting system.

How to Network

Networking is easier than you think. You already have a social network (relatives, personal friends, classmates, etc.). Now you need to expand your personal network into a job campaign network. Remember, everyone who has a job has been in your situation, and most successful people are willing to help. Here is how to develop your job campaign network.

- **Get organized.** Keep track of every contact. Look at the Networking Directory form on page 71. It provides the means to create your own personal networking directory. Update your directory daily.

- **Get the word out that you are searching for a job.** Ask friends, relatives, professors and people who graduated last year about opportunities where they work. Contact people you know who work for firms where you would like to work. Ask for leads and referrals. Try to obtain at least two or three names from each person.

- **Contact trade and professional organizations for job banks, membership directories, newsletter listings, etc.** Obtain lists of company contacts from college placement offices. Get lists of established professionals from college alumni offices.

- **Target individuals in a field or company you would like to get into and ask for an information (not a job) interview.** Call key people whose names you have obtained and ask for an appointment to learn more about their specific industry. You will be surprised how effective this approach is. People are flattered to be asked for advice. In addition, they will usually give you names of friends, acquaintances and firms to call as well as ideas for you to try.

When You Request an Information Interview

When calling to schedule an information interview, remember to:

- **Introduce yourself.**

- **Give the name of the person who referred you.**

Terry McMillan, author of **Disappearing Acts** *and* **Waiting to Exhale,** *worked as a word processor for a law firm while writing her first book,* **Mama.**

- **State that you are requesting an appointment** for a 30-minute information interview.

- **Ask to arrange** a mutually convenient time.

Tips for Successful Networking

- **Script what you are going to say** on the phone (see Part Six, pages 93–94).

- **Ask a secretary for assistance** getting to the person you are calling. If this doesn't work, call before 8:30 A.M. or after 5:30 P.M., when the person is more likely to answer his or her own phone, or leave a message in their voice mailbox (see page 97).

- **If the person has voice mail,** leave a message containing the information described above. For example, you could call the targeted individual and say: "Hello, my name is Virginia Union. I was referred to you by Cary Collins. I'm interested in the public relations industry. I'm calling to ask if you might have thirty minutes to meet me. I'm looking for information on the various aspects of the industry and some advice on how to become a part of it."

- **If the person's answer is "yes," say,** "When would it be convenient to meet?"

- **If the answer is negative, say,** "Could you possibly recommend someone else I could call?"

- **Then thank your contact** for his or her interest and kindness.

Conducting an Information Interview

The objectives of an information interview are to learn more about a field and to obtain contacts for job opportunities. This referral information is the key to getting results.

The Questions to Ask

- How did you get started in this business?

- What are the positive aspects of being in this business?

- If you had to do it again, what would you do differently?

- Where do you see the industry heading now and in the future?

- What and where are the current career opportunities in the industry?

- Is there a trade association representing the industry?

- Is there someone with the association I should talk with?

- Who would you recommend I contact regarding job opportunities?

- Is there anything else I should know about the industry?

- What would you do if you were in my situation?

Some Helpful Hints

- Relax, this is not a job interview—it will be fun.

- Prepare questions in advance and take notes.

- Bring a résumé and ask for comments, suggestions, ideas.

- Ask for referrals to other people in the career field.

- Leave your résumé for possible follow-up.

- Send a thank-you note, and keep the person posted on your progress.

- Update your Networking Directory every day.

Electronic Networking

If you are shy, hesitant to make telephone calls, reluctant to ask friends for referrals and have a personal computer, electronic networking may be a comfortable route for you to take. It can be fast, effective, and if used properly, relatively inexpensive. You can network across the nation from the privacy of your own home without embarrassment. And, the computer never loses patience, although you might.

The key to electronic networking is to find a special interest group or forum that matches your career or job field. All of the online services (see page 49) make listings of these groups available online and off. Forums include business, engineering, health, legal and hundreds of other subjects. Just sign on and introduce yourself. There are even practice forums to help you gain confidence and build skills in using the forums.

Keep in mind some caution signs to prevent you from getting sideswiped on the road to your dream job:

- **Your computer, like your telephone, is a communications tool.** It is only as good as you are at using it.

- **Electronic networking may get you more or less exposure than you want or need.** You may be overwhelmed with responses that are not job-related and underwhelmed with job leads.

- **Electronic networking doesn't altogether replace traditional approaches.** There is no substitute for face-to-face contact, followed closely by voice contact. Eventually, you will have to get off-line and deal with people in the "real," not "virtual" world.

Suggested Reading

- *Effective Networking*
Venda Raye-Johnson, Crisp Publications

- *Electronic Job Search Revolution*
  Joyce Lain Kennedy and Thomas J. Morrow, John Wiley & Sons, Inc.

- *Information Interviewing: What It Is and How to Use It in Your Career*
  Martha Stoodley, Garrett Park Press

- *It's Who You Know*
  Cynthia Chin-Lee, Pfeiffer & Company

- *Network Your Way to Your Next Job...Fast*
  Clyde Lowstuter and David Robertson, McGraw-Hill

How to Use Your Networking Directory

The following worksheet will help you keep track of your personal network of contacts. Reproduce one of these two-page forms for each letter of the alphabet (mark them A through Z) and place them in your job-search organizing notebook to produce your own Networking Directory.

Record the date of the telephone call/meeting, the person's name, title, company, address and phone numbers, who they were referred by, who they referred you to, and when you sent a thank-you letter. Use as many blocks as you need to accommodate all the information.

You may also want to place notes of conversations with your networking contacts in your notebook. Label each set of notes with the person's name, address and phone number, and file them alphabetically (by the first initial of each last name) after the appropriate networking directory worksheet. Or, you could also create a folder for each networking contact.

If you learn that a networking contact has a job to offer, reenter that information in the Action Log (see page 89) and on a Job Prospect Profile (see page 106).

Your Networking Directory will serve as a permanent record for continuing use during your career. You will find it a valuable reference if you keep it current as time passes.

COPY

Networking Directory

Date of Contact	Person's Name and Title	Telephone Number	Company's Name and Address	Date of Thank You	Referred By	Provided Referrals To

WHEN YOU MARKET YOURSELF

THE MARKETING PROCESS

A job campaign involves marketing, whether we recognize it or not. Marketing is a process that provides all the supporting resources to sell a product or service. In a job campaign, you are the product. You must market yourself to the prospective employer. That means making sure that he or she clearly understands your ability to serve the organization's needs. Given that measurement of success, let's see how you can market yourself. The marketing process consists of these four functions:

- **Presentation:** Offering your skills and experience as beneficial to the prospective employer.

- **Promotion:** Creating awareness of your capabilities.

- **Positioning:** Gaining a preference or competitive advantage.

- **Pricing:** Getting what you are worth in today's market.

Action Words to Make Your Point

Achieve	Market
Analyze	Monitor
Attain	Motivate
Calculate	Negotiate
Coach	Obtain
Compose	Organize
Conduct	Originate
Contribute	Plan
Create	Prepare
Design	Present
Develop	Produce
Direct	Promote
Enhance	Propose
Evaluate	Recommend
Expedite	Research
Forecast	Resolve
Generate	Schedule
Identify	Sell
Improve	Simplify
Initiate	Specify
Install	Start
Instruct	Supervise
Integrate	Teach
Interview	Train
Investigate	Translate
Make	Write

PRESENTATION
(You Are What Your Résumé Says You Are)

Your résumé presents your qualifications to a prospective employer. It must convince him or her that you are a qualified candidate. Its objective is to get you an interview. Your résumé should:

- **Highlight** the benefits you offer.

- **Show** how your capabilities satisfy the employer's requirements.

- **Differentiate** you from the crowd by emphasizing your accomplishments.

The Contents

Best Approach
Try to obtain a copy of a job description and tailor your résumé to the specific job requirements. This is easy if you have access to a personal computer and a laser printer. Otherwise, go with a generic résumé.

Skills
Match your skills to the specific job requirements, consistent with your job objective. Use key words that describe your skills succinctly, and that prospective employers will relate to and their résumé scanning systems will recognize.

Objective
Your job objective may be stated in your résumé or in your cover letter. Regardless, your objective should adhere to the following formula. Describe the type of position you want, the type of organization you want to work in or the area of interest you want to pursue, the skills you want to use, and any experience that you want to highlight.

Education

List the names of educational institutions, degrees, dates awarded, honors and awards (GPA if 3.5 or above), and the percentage of educational costs that were paid through grants, scholarships, jobs, cooperatives, and student loans.

Experience

Focus on your ABCs:

- **Accomplishments.** Activities with tangible results.

- **Benefits.** How you satisfy the specific needs of the potential employer.

- **Capabilities.** What you can produce or deliver.

Language

- **Be brief,** accurate and focused.

- **Write in the first person** without the pronoun "I." For example, use "produced" rather than "I produced."

- **Look for key words in the job ad** or position description. Then use the same or similar key words in your skills summary.

- **Use action verbs** such as "achieve" (if you're referring to your current job), "achieved" (if referring to a previous job). The list on page 74 may help you find the right words.

- **Make all your words work for you.** Despite the emphasis on verbs, the nouns count, too.

- **Avoid referring to "activities," "duties" or "responsibilities."** Replace with your ABCs, discussed earlier.

After being expelled from Princeton University, R.W. Apple, reporter for the New York Times, served in the Army. There he wrote speeches, testimonials and other pieces for the commanding general.

Nina Totenberg, broadcast journalist with National Public Radio and ABC's Nightline, dropped out of Boston University to find work as a journalist. In her first job, she rewrote recipes and wedding announcements.

Patricia Ireland, president of the National Organization of Women, earned a bachelor's degree in German from the University of Tennessee.

Design

The key is to present your skills and experience as effectively as possible, depending on who you are trying to impress. For starters, your résumé should look like a published document—uncluttered with plenty of white space. And, it should be suitable for today's electronic scanning technology.

Three résumé formats—*chronological, functional* and a *combined chronological/functional*—are presented in this book for your consideration (see pages 80–82). The chronological format is probably the most widely used and most recognizable format. It allows the reader to find pertinent information quickly and effectively. You'll want to use a functional format if you don't already have work experience. You'll be able to concentrate on your skills rather than your experience, and you won't jeopardize your position as a job candidate. The combination of these formats highlights your job experiences and the skills you have gained in these positions.

Regardless of format, use just one page. More detailed information can be provided during the interview. Later on in your career, when you have gained more experience, your résumé can be longer.

Administrative Details

Ask a placement or personnel professional to critique your résumé and suggest any appropriate improvements.

If you use a personal computer to tailor your résumé to specific job requirements, be sure to use a laser printer to produce the best quality. If you don't have a laser printer, take your résumé on diskette to someone who does.

If you use a generic résumé, you may want to have it professionally printed. Request at least 200 to 300 copies of your résumé. It isn't cost-effective to print fewer than 100.

In either case, you will generally want to choose a

heavy, high-quality paper. Avoid eye-catching colored paper and go with natural white, which facilitates electronic scanning.

Many prospective employers are using computerized résumé scanning and tracking systems to deal with the many résumés they receive. Employers can search the resulting data base by key words relevant to the jobs they are trying to fill. For more on how to format your résumé to make sure that a computer can read it, consult the checklist on page 79 and the resources listed below, and see the résumé samples on pages 80–82.

Always send your résumé with a cover letter tailored to the particular job. Direct it to the attention of the specific person (name and title) who will be responsible for hiring you.

If you mail your résumé, enclose it in a sufficiently large envelope that you needn't fold the résumé.

Suggested Reading

- *From College to Career:*
  Entry-Level Résumés for Any Major
  Donald Asher, Ten Speed Press

- *Résumés That Work*
  Loretta D. Foxman, John Wiley & Sons

- *Résumés That Knock 'Em Dead*
  Martin Yate, Adams Publishing

- *Electronic Résumé Revolution*
  Joyce Lain Kennedy and Thomas J. Morrow

- *Electronic Résumés for the New Job Market*
  Peter D. Weddle, Impact Publications

Tony Hillerman, author of the Jim Chee and Joe Leaphorn mysteries, wrote Purina Pig Chow commercials for a radio station in Oklahoma City.

Résumé Do's and Don'ts

Do:

- Make it easy for someone to get a quick assessment of your skills.

- Include succinct descriptions of your achievements.

- Emphasize your most significant skills and accomplishments in a prominent position.

- Link your skills to the requirements of the job you're seeking through the use of key words and relevant examples.

Make your resume scanner-friendly.

- Describe your skills using key words placed just below your name (see the sample résumés on pages 80–82).

- Use a sans serif typeface, such as Helvetica, to give each character a distinct, machine-readable edge.

- Use a type font size of at least 10 points.

- Avoid italics, script and underlining.

- Do not use graphics or shading.

Don't include:

- Misspelled words and typographical errors.

- Sloppy grammar or syntax.

- Confused chronology.

- Personal data (age, marital status, current or previous salaries, or reference to health conditions).

- Religious or political affiliations.

- Names of references.

Résumé Checklist

The following checklist has been designed to assist you in evaluating your résumé. Make sure your résumé meets the following criteria. (Go through this checklist each time you change your résumé.)

Appearance
- ❑ is visually pleasing
- ❑ is easy to read
- ❑ looks like a published document
- ❑ can be scanned electronically

Contact Information
- ❑ is clearly presented at top
- ❑ includes current address
- ❑ includes telephone number(s) where you can be reached during business hours (9 A.M. to 5 P.M.)

Skills
- ❑ are consistent with objective
- ❑ should match job requirements
- ❑ are substantiated by experience
- ❑ are described using "key words"

Objective
- ❑ includes type of job you seek
- ❑ includes type of organization
- ❑ emphasizes your strongest skills

Education
- ❑ lists most recent degree; date or anticipated date of graduation
- ❑ lists other relevant education certificate programs, short courses
- ❑ includes name and location of university, college or training institution
- ❑ names major, minor, or area(s) of concentration or interest

- ❑ lists honors and awards
- ❑ mentions GPA if 3.5 or above
- ❑ tells percentage of education you paid through jobs, grants, scholarships and student loans

Experience
Each paid, volunteer, intern, or co-op experience relevant to your objective that you list includes:
- ❑ title, organization name, city, state and country (if not U.S.)
- ❑ dates position held
- ❑ position description that highlights skills, relevant accomplishments and benefits you offer
- ❑ specific examples of successes to substantiate your objective

Extracurricular Activities
- ❑ list offices held, including title and organization
- ❑ emphasize leadership roles
- ❑ include pertinent memberships and affiliations
- ❑ include sports participation
- ❑ list ROTC training
- ❑ present certifications, such as those for paralegal, emergency medical technician or lifesaving
- ❑ include significant papers, relevant conferences attended, foreign study, and language fluency

Sample Résumé—Chronological Format

Virginia C. Union
2323 Sullivan Ballou Avenue, Bull Run, VA 22090, Phone (703) 555–1234

Skills
- Research and reporting, interviewing, writing and editing
- Meet deadlines. Obtain quality results working with other people
- Proficient in Microsoft Word (for Mac), Pagemaker and Freehand
- Experience with online information services

Objective   Obtain a position as a writer with a public relations firm utilizing my degree in English, my word processing and desktop publishing skills, and my staff writing experience.

Education   **Virginia Commonwealth University,** Richmond, Virginia, Bachelor of Arts in English, May 1997, cum laude. GPA: 3.5. Fifty percent of education paid through scholarships, jobs, student loans and internships. Honors include Dean's List and Lee Foundation scholarship.

Experience   **Staff Writer,** Environmental Services, Inc., Washington, D.C., July 1997–Present.
Research and write proposals and project reports for submittal to the U.S. Environmental Protection Agency.

Campus Correspondent, "The Richmond News Leader," Richmond, Virginia, August 1994–May 1997.
Wrote feature articles for the Young Virginians section.

Staff Writer, "New Age for Seniors," Richmond, Virginia, January 1995–January 1997.
Wrote feature articles and calendar of events. Helped plan monthly issues. Typeset editorial and ad copy.

Assistant Editor, Telecon Database Marketing Company, Cedar Rapids, Iowa, June–August 1994.
Coordinated a staff of volunteer reporters; wrote, edited, designed and distributed internal company newsletter.

References   Available upon request.

Sample Résumé—Functional Format

Virginia C. Union
2323 Sullivan Ballou Avenue, Bull Run, VA 22090, Phone (703) 555–1234

Skills
- Research and reporting, interviewing, writing and editing
- Meet deadlines. Obtain quality results working with other people
- Proficient in Microsoft Word (for Mac), Pagemaker and Freehand
- Experience with online information services

Objective   Obtain a position as a writer with a public relations firm utilizing my degree in English, my word processing and desktop publishing skills, and my staff writing experience.

Education   Virginia Commonwealth University, Richmond, Virginia, Bachelor of Arts in English, May 1997, cum laude. GPA: 3.5. Fifty percent of education paid through scholarships, jobs, student loans and internships. Honors include Dean's List and Lee Foundation scholarship.

Experience   **Research.** Currently perform library and computer online information searches for own use in writing proposals and technical reports for environmental services firm.

Interviewing. Conducted more than one hundred personal interviews with students, educators, professionals and business representatives as campus correspondent for Richmond, Virginia newspaper. Obtains desired results with pleasant personality, open mind and quick thinking.

Writing. Wrote more than 250 feature and news articles, newsletters, proposals and reports as staff writer and newspaper intern reporter. Writing samples available upon request.

Editorial Services/Desktop Publishing. Published internal company newsletter utilizing a staff of summer volunteer reporters. Managed editing, layout, design and distribution as Assistant Editor. Used Macintosh Microsoft Word, Pagemaker and Freehand.

References   Available upon request.

Sample Résumé—Combined Chronological and Functional Format

Virginia C. Union
2323 Sullivan Ballou Avenue, Bull Run, VA 22090, Phone (703) 555–1234

Skills
- Research and reporting, interviewing, writing and editing
- Meet deadlines. Obtain quality results working with other people
- Proficient in Microsoft Word (for Mac), Pagemaker and Freehand
- Experience with online information services

Objective   Obtain a position as a writer with a public relations firm utilizing my degree in English, my word processing and desktop publishing skills, and my staff writing experience.

Education   **Virginia Commonwealth University,** Richmond, Virginia, Bachelor of Arts in English, May 1997, cum laude. GPA: 3.5. Fifty percent of education paid through scholarships, jobs, student loans and internships. Honors include Dean's List and Lee Foundation scholarship.

Accomplishments

Interviewing. Conducted more than one hundred personal interviews with professionals, students, educators and business leaders as campus correspondent for Richmond, Virginia, newspaper.

Writing. Wrote more than 250 feature and news articles, newsletters, proposals and reports as staff writer and newspaper intern reporter. Writing samples available upon request.

Word Processing/Desktop Publishing. Produced more than 200 pages of documents using Macintosh Microsoft Word, Pagemaker and Freehand.

Experience   **Staff Writer,** Environmental Services, Inc., Washington, D.C., July 1997–Present.

Campus Correspondent, "The Richmond News Leader," Richmond, Virginia, Aug. 1994–May 1997.

Staff Writer, "New Age for Seniors," Richmond, Virginia, Jan. 1995–Jan. 1997.

Assistant Editor, Telecon Database Marketing Company, Cedar Rapids, Iowa, June–Aug. 1994.

References   Available upon request.

RÉSUMÉ COVER LETTERS

A cover letter serves as an introduction to your résumé and an opportunity to say something specific about how you qualify for the specific job. Organize your letter as follows:

- **Paragraph 1:** State objective, benefits you can provide and the source of your referral.

- **Paragraph 2:** Indicate why you are interested in the position, how you are qualified for it and why the company (or job if known) appeals to you.

- **Paragraph 3:** Request a specific form of response, state your next step and thank the reader for his or her time and consideration.

The sample cover letter on the next page illustrates the recommended approach.

Suggested Reading

- *Sure-Hire Cover Letters*
  Robbie Miller Kaplan, AMACOM

- *Dynamite Cover Letters*
  Ronald and Caryl Krannich,
  Impact Publications

Sample Résumé Cover Letter

Virginia C. Union
2323 Sullivan Ballou Avenue
Bull Run, VA 22090
(703) 555–1234

July 1, 1997

Ms. Jill Senate
Director of Communications
Washington Associates, Inc.
1801 Pennsylvania Avenue, N.W.
Washington, DC 20000

Dear Ms. Senate:

I would like to explore the possibility of joining your organization as a staff writer. My degree in English, word processing skills and staff writing experience qualify me for such a position. I was referred to you by Ms. Jane Wilson of the Public Relations Society of America.

I am seeking a position that will utilize and expand my writing skills. My specific experience in writing proposals and reports for the U.S. Environmental Protection Agency should be of interest since your clients include chemical manufacturers. Also, my work in the environmental field fits your organization's work with the petroleum industry.

My résumé summarizes my qualifications. In addition, I would appreciate the opportunity to discuss with you in more detail how I can assist your organization. If I do not hear from you by July 12th, I will call you to arrange an appointment. In the meantime, thank you for your consideration of my qualifications.

Sincerely,

Virginia C. Union

Enclosure

PROMOTION
(Getting Noticed)

Promotion is making an audience of prospective employers aware of your qualifications. Part Six discusses promotion in more detail, but here are some nontraditional ways to accomplish this task:

- **Fax your résumé** to a very targeted audience (see page 102) or create a home page for yourself—in effect, a personal electronic billboard—on the Internet's World-Wide Web. (See page 50.)

- **List yourself** in appropriate trade association newsletters and job banks under "Positions Wanted." (See page 56.)

- **Prepare 3 x 5 or rotary file** (i.e., Rolodex) "leave behind" cards that contain your name, address and phone number on the front and your job objective and skills from your résumé on the back. You can get these printed by most printers. Carry some with you at all times, and give one to anyone who may have reason to contact you later about a job.

- **Be your own working advertisement** by working as a temp. A temporary job as a clerk, receptionist or courier provides valuable experiences, contacts and references. Sometimes the temporary job will lead directly to a permanent position.

- **Volunteer for organizations and activities,** such as golf tournaments or runs for charity, with business sponsors or relationships. This will increase your visibility and personal contacts.

- **Participate actively in your college alumni association.** If an employer has had success with graduates of your college, you start off with a positive perception. And alumni can refer you to their customers, vendors and competitors.

Kirstie Alley, actress, worked as an interior decorator in Kansas City.

Marlee Matlin, actress and star of the critically acclaimed movie "Children of a Lesser God," studied criminal justice at Harper Junior College and wanted to join the police.

An MBA That Pays

In 1996, MBAs with technical undergraduate degrees and more than four years of experience were offered the highest average salary—$69,344—of all graduate students.

POSITIONING
(Preparation Finding Opportunity)

Positioning (also known as networking) is arranging to be known in the right place at the right time when a job opportunity develops. How can you do this? Here is a proven approach for strategic career positioning:

- **Join an association** that has a business/educational orientation rather than a pure social function. Every profession has such an organization. Many have student memberships. Check with the appropriate association to find a chapter in your area.

- **Participate in the association's activities.** Volunteer to be on a committee. View the time as an investment in your future career.

- **Be patient.** You probably won't land a job from the first meeting. It takes time to build rapport and respect with the other members. Above all, don't oversell yourself. Just work hard for the mutual benefit of all the members.

- **Maintain reasonable expectations.** The rewards will come in small packages. The one great job opportunity may come after a series of little learning experiences. But it will be worth it.

- **Send thank-you notes for any assistance you receive.** It's amazing how few people do this. Yet, it always makes a good impression. Guess whose name is going to pop into someone's mind when a job opportunity does arise?

For more on the job-hunting resources offered by trade and professional associations, see the discussion beginning on page 60. Additional approaches to gain a competitive advantage are discussed in Part Six, "Job Campaign Tactics That Work."

PRICING
(Dollars and Sense)

What you will be offered for your services will depend upon the ability/resources of the employer, your qualifications, the job salary range, location and current market conditions. To get some idea of what different jobs pay, you can obtain salary data from the following sources:

- Trade and professional association surveys

- *National Association of Colleges and Employers Salary Survey*

- *American Almanac of Jobs and Salaries*

- Salary Guide, *http://www.espan.com/salary/salary.html*

- Department of Labor Area Salary Surveys

- Professionals in the career field

- Previous year's graduates

The next step is to develop a monthly expense budget to see how much gross income you will need to live. This will depend on where you live and your spending habits. Estimate your take-home pay to be approximately 65% of your gross pay. Be sure to include a reserve for the inevitable emergencies. Then compare your needs with published salary ranges to determine your personal salary requirements.

Salary negotiations are discussed in Part Seven, "Interviewing For First Place." Surviving on your income is discussed in Part Three, "Planning Your Job Campaign."

By Comparison

In 1996, candidates for master's degrees in physical education received the lowest average salary offer—$25,364—of all graduate students, followed by those with a master's in humanities ($27,069) and elementary education ($27,118).

How to Use Your Action Log

Use this Action Log to track your contacts with prospective employers and the dates of your correspondence, phone calls and interviews with them. Be as detailed and organized as possible—it will make your follow-up easier and more effective.

Reproduce this form for each letter of the alphabet (mark them "A" through "Z") and place them in your job-search organizing notebook. You may wish to file your Job Prospect Profile worksheets alphabetically (by the first initial of each person's last name) after the appropriate Action Log sheet.

Action Log

Name of Company, Name of Contact and Telephone Number	Dates Résumés Sent	Dates of Telephone Calls	Dates Correspondence Sent	Dates of Interviews

JOB CAMPAIGN TACTICS THAT WORK

THE PRINCIPLES OF SUCCESS

View your job campaign as an opportunity to meet different people, learn new skills and experience new adventures. The result will be an exciting and rewarding experience. Enjoy the process of becoming a wiser person.

Your job campaign strategy is the big picture, and it focuses your efforts toward your career goal. Your job campaign tactics are the day-to-day actions that produce the results. Which is more important: strategy or tactics? Both. It's the combination of the two that will make your job campaign successful. Make day-to-day adjustments to your game plan. You will write the script as you move ahead. You are in charge!

The job campaign tactics presented in Part Six are proven techniques designed to help you outwit and outmaneuver your competition. However, it is up to you to outwork your competitors to get the job you want. In addition, you may want to keep the following principles in mind as you implement your job campaign tactics.

Compete to Win

Only the winner gets the job. Never settle for average. Polish your job-search skills every day. Improve your marketing materials as you learn. Always ask yourself, "How can I do it any better?" Then do it better.

Maintain a Positive Attitude

Rejection is normal when competing for a job. Do not let rejection lead to discouragement. Always obtain something of value from each call, contact or interview. Then build on each and every small victory. A series of small victories will increase your confidence and lead to ultimate success in your job campaign.

The Difference a Degree Makes

Here's how the unemployment rate in 1995 varied by level of education among people aged 25 and older. (The overall rate of unemployment for this group was 4.3%.)

college degree	**2.4%**
some college, but no degree	**4.3%**
high school degree	**4.8%**
no high school degree	**9.0%**

Do Your Homework

Preparation gives you a competitive edge. A display of intimate knowledge about an industry, a company, a job or the interviewer is crucial to getting the job you want. Invest the time to do the required research. It will pay dividends.

Work Harder and Smarter Than Others

There is no substitute for working *hard* and *smart*. Working hard turns up unexpected opportunities. Working smart eliminates time-wasting diversions. When in doubt, *act*. Do something simple, and then you can expand on it.

Be Persistent

Take full responsibility for getting the job you want, and never give up. One more phone call may lead to exactly the job opportunity you want. One more visit may produce an acquaintance who can help you. One more rejection letter may motivate you to change tactics for better results.

COMMUNICATE TO GET RESULTS

The Telephone

Next to face-to-face contact, the telephone is the most personal means available to find a job. Every call you make is an opportunity to talk with a prospective employer, to discover a new job opening or to obtain a referral. Your approach in the initial telephone contact can have a positive impact on your chances to obtain what you want from the call. Try these suggestions:

- **Complete at least ten calls per day.** You will be amazed at the results.

- **Develop your own telephone personality,** but always be pleasant, courteous and confident. Smile when you speak; the listener will hear it.

- **Prepare a brief outline** for each call and rehearse. Then relax, call and have a friendly conversation.

- **Think in terms of short statements** covering what you want to accomplish.

- **Call around 8 A.M. and after 5 P.M.** if you want to avoid secretaries.

- **Get to know every secretary by name.** He or she is the gatekeeper who can assure or deny access to the person with whom you need to speak. Ask to receive information about the company (annual reports, newsletters, brochures) and, if possible, a copy of the job description.

- **Voice mail is a great way** to speak directly to the proper person. Use it to leave concise messages.

Robert Fulghum, minister and author of Everything I Need to Know I Learned in Kindergarten, *joined IBM's management training program.*

- **Take notes** during each telephone conversation. If appropriate, attach the notes to the Job Prospect form in this section. Date all notes.

- **If you get a negative response,** ask for referrals to other people, companies or organizations.

- **All calls have value.** You just have to find it. Always ask for referrals, referrals and referrals.

Telephone Inquiry Procedure for Success (TIPS)

Objective

Use the telephone to arrange an information interview and to obtain other information and job leads.

Finding the Right Person

If you don't have the name of a key executive in the area where you wish to work, ask the receptionist for it. For example, you might want the name of the general manager, vice president of sales or the customer service director. Write down the information, and ask to speak with that person.

Dealing with the Secretary

- **Say:** "Hello, this is Virginia Union, may I speak with Mr. (Name)?"

- **If you are asked who you represent, say:** "Myself."

- **If you are asked about the subject of the call, say:** "I have been asked by (name of referral) to talk with Mr. (Name) about a personal matter."

- **If you are asked about the subject of the call and were not referred, just say:** "A personal matter."

- **If the executive is not available,** leave your name and number for the person to return your call. And, be sure to get the name of the secretary so you can address him or her by name the next time you call.

- **Note all calls in your Action Log** for future reference or in your Networking Directory, if you're working in that stage of the game (see pages 71 and 89).

- **If you are talking from your home,** use a longer telephone cord. That way you can stand or move about, which may relieve initial anxiety. However, you may have to sit down to take notes.

- **Use voice mail or an answering machine** to receive messages while you are away from the phone.

When You Reach Your Target

- **Say:** "Hello, Ms. (Name), this is Virginia Union. I appreciate you talking with me today. I know you must receive many calls, so I'll be brief. I'm a recent graduate of Virginia Commonwealth University with a Bachelor's degree in English. My goal is to be a staff writer with a company such as yours taking advantage of my writing experience and desktop publishing skills. I'd appreciate an opportunity to talk with you about how I might help you improve your corporate communications."

- **If the executive is hesitant,** point out that you will need only 20 minutes of time, that you will bring your résumé with you to save time and that you would like to schedule the appointment at his or her convenience.

- **If the executive wants to refer you to the personnel manager,** ask if it is possible to meet with the executive first to obtain some background information.

- **If the executive says there are no new positions available at this time, ask for an information interview or referrals. Say:** "Would it be possible to have an information interview to learn more about your industry?" Or: "Do you know of any of your associates who may need someone with my skills and experience?"

- **If nothing seems to be working, say:** "What do you suggest for someone in my situation?"

- **If you reach a complete dead end, smile and say:** "Thank you," and move on.

- **Send an appropriate follow-up letter** (see the following sample).

Sample Phone Follow-Up Cover Letter

Virginia C. Union
2323 Sullivan Ballou Avenue
Bull Run, VA 22090
(703) 555–1234

July 10, 1997

Ms. Jill Senate
Director of Communications
Washington Associates, Inc.
1801 Pennsylvania Avenue, N.W.
Washington, DC 20000

Dear Ms. Senate:

Thank you for speaking with me on the phone today about my interest in joining your firm as staff writer. I have enclosed my résumé as you requested.

As we discussed, I am seeking a position in which I can apply and expand my writing skills. My specific experience in writing proposals and reports to the U.S. Environmental Protection Agency should be of interest because your clients include chemical manufacturers. Also, my work in the environmental field fits your organization's business focus.

My résumé summarizes my qualifications. In addition, I would appreciate the opportunity to meet with you to discuss in more detail how I can assist your organization. If I do not hear from you by July 19th, I will call you to arrange an appointment. In the meantime, thank you for your consideration of my qualifications.

Sincerely,

Virginia C. Union

Enclosure

The Fax

In some cases, you may be asked to fax your résumé. In other situations, using a fax for delivery can get you special attention over other candidates. For example, you may want to fax your résumé in response to an ad and mail a printed copy at the same time. Or you may want to selectively distribute your résumé by fax to prospective employers (see page 102). Always fax a cover letter with your résumé. And always call to confirm that the fax was received. Fax machines are available in many office supply, packaging and quick-print stores.

Voice Mail

Voice mail is a sophisticated telephone answering system that allows you to leave messages directly with the person you are calling without playing telephone tag or going through a secretary. Incoming touch-tone phone calls are directed to the recipient's voice mail box, where you hear a personalized greeting and are requested to leave a detailed message. This is a perfect opportunity to present your clear and concise message.

Sometimes, a fully automated system will ask you to input the extension of the person you are calling. If this is the case, wait for a live person to come on the line and ask for the person's extension. If you land in "voice mail jail," where you are cycled from one recorded message to another, call information and attempt to get a direct number.

Some colleges, universities and corporations offer voice mail job lines. These are recorded job listings with the actual voices of employers stating their specific job requirements. The services are available 24 hours a day, 7 days a week. If you are dealing with larger companies, trade associations or college career services, ask whether they have a voice mail job line.

Anita Roddick, founder of The Body Shop, purveyor of personal care products, studied English, history and aesthetics at Newton Park College of Education in England and wanted to become a teacher.

Personal Cover Letters

Most generic résumés accompanied by generic cover letters fail to get interviews. Cover letters and résumés usually don't get read beyond the first few lines, and the generic ones tend to get disqualified within 20 seconds. If you elect to use the cover letter approach, you should be prepared to do three things:

1. **Persuade** the reader to read your entire résumé and then talk with you by making your cover letter focused and to the point. (See Part Five, "When You Market Yourself," for tips on how to present yourself and your correspondence effectively.)

2. **Personalize** your cover letter.

3. **Follow up** with a phone call within five days.

Also, keep in mind the following:

- **A personal letter should be just that**—a letter with a personal flavor. You want the reader to think he or she is getting the only copy of this letter, not a much-mailed form letter.

- **Use simple, straightforward language** to let the reader know what you want.

- **Write in terms of how the reader will benefit** from doing what you ask in the letter.

Sample Personal Cover Letter (With Résumé)

Virginia C. Union
2323 Sullivan Ballou Avenue
Bull Run, VA 22090
(703) 555–1234

July 10, 1997

Ms. Jill Senate
Director of Communications
Washington Associates, Inc.
1801 Pennsylvania Avenue, N.W.
Washington, DC 20000

Dear Ms. Senate:

I would like to explore the possibility of joining your organization as a staff writer. My degree in English, word processing skills and staff writing experience qualify me as a potential asset to your firm.

I am seeking a position in which I can apply and expand my writing skills. My specific experience in writing proposals and reports to the U.S. Environmental Protection Agency should be of interest because your clients include chemical manufacturers. Also, my work in the environmental field fits your organization's business focus.

My résumé summarizes my qualifications. In addition, I would appreciate the opportunity to meet with you and discuss in more detail how I can assist your organization. If I do not hear from you by July 19th, I will call you to arrange an appointment. In the meantime, thank you for your consideration of my qualifications.

Sincerely,

Virginia C. Union

Enclosure

ANSWERING ADVERTISEMENTS

In today's world, most business communications are via the telephone, fax and e-mail. However, some of you may be more comfortable using real mail. And, sometimes you must send your response to a classified ad to a post office box. Even so, always try to follow up a letter with a phone call. Otherwise, you are probably wasting your time. Here are some guidelines that will enable you to get the most out of your mailings.

The key to success in responding to a classified ad is to separate yourself from the crowd by matching your qualifications to the ad's requirements. Some important job information will be presented in the ad itself. Now you need to:

- **Call and find out as much as possible** about the job, the company, and the qualifications of the person the company wants. Try to obtain a copy of the job description and the name of the hiring executive from the personnel manager.

- **If you are told to "please send your résumé as directed,"** explain that you are just trying to respond effectively so you won't be wasting the personnel manager's time.

- **Tailor your résumé and/or cover letter** to the job requirements. Match the key words in the ad to your key qualifications.

- **Write a cover letter that shows a special interest in or unique qualification** for the job, and refer to your telephone conversation.

- **Check your cover letter and résumé for mistakes.** Then ask someone with an eye for detail to check it. Then check it again.

- **File copies of all letters** in your job-search organizing notebook for quick and effective follow-up. Remember, cover letters are a good place to jot down notes or directions while you are on the phone.

- **Call the hiring executive to give a "heads-up"** that your résumé is coming. Use your telephone approach to get a commitment from the hiring executive to look specifically for your résumé and to send you a copy of the job description if you don't have it.

- **If no corporate name is given** (a "blind ad"), call the newspaper's classified section and ask for the name of the advertiser. Some states require that such information be furnished upon request.

More on the Sexes

On average, in 1995 men with high school degrees earned $31,063 and those with associate degrees earned $37,628, while women with bachelor's degrees earned $33,666.

IF YOU USE MAILING LISTS

Shotgun mailings and faxes are a waste of time and money. The key to success is to target your audience. The more precise your target audience, the better your chance for successful results.

- **Obtain lists of people by job function** from trade association membership and other industry directories (see page 48).

- **Check each list** and eliminate companies you are not really interested in due to size, location, etc.

- **Focus your mailings** to the specific people in the companies you have targeted.

- **Never** mail a résumé to a company without an individual's name and title.

- **Tailor your résumé and cover letter** to address a precise job function in the targeted company.

- **Use your Action Log** (see page 89) for tracking your mailings.

Fax Services

Once in a while, you may want to fax your résumé to a select group of prospective employers. All of the rules for mailing lists, discussed above, apply to faxes, as well. You may also want to prepare and use an attention-getting cover sheet that broadcasts your message in big, bold print and graphics. As always, the key to getting results is prompt follow-up.

Fax services are available from office supply, packaging and business-service stores, such as Kinko's and Mail Boxes, Etc. The cost for this type of service averages about $1 per page for local service and $2 per page for long-distance locations. Such services typically charge nothing for the cover sheet and provide a confirmation report that your faxes were successfully transmitted.

LEAVING MILITARY SERVICE

If you are leaving military service after three or thirty years, you're in for some culture shock. Half the officers and a third of the enlisted men who leave the service are still unemployed after six months. To avoid joining this club, follow these suggestions:

- **Don't depend on your military accomplishments** to earn you a job. You are starting over in a new ball game. Let this guide teach you the new rules.

- **Use the career and alumni offices** in the college or university where you received your degree or near where you live to provide information and leads.

- **Many national search firms have specialists** working with former military officers. A few firms specialize in this area. (See reference to *The Directory of Executive Recruiters* on page 64.)

- **You must have a civilian résumé** to translate your military accomplishments into corporate terminology (see "Suggested Reading," below).

Suggested Reading

- *The Career Discovery Project*
  Gerald M. Sturmann, PhD, Bantam Doubleday

- *From Army Green to Corporate Gray*
- *From Navy Blue to Corporate Gray*
- *From Air Force Blue to Corporate Gray*
  Carl Savino, Major, USAR, and Ronald Krannich, PhD, Impact Publications

Michael Eisner, chairman of Disney, earned a degree in English and theatre from Denison University, in Ohio. In his first studio job, he worked as a page with NBC for the summer.

Cindy Crawford, model, was awarded a full-tuition scholarship to study chemical engineering at Northwestern University. She left after one semester.

Job Intelligence Gathering

Sometimes uncommon methods provide a competitive advantage when competing for a job. Try these ideas if you are willing to attempt a different approach:

- **Ask friends to search employee bulletin boards** where they work for internal job listings.

- **Call the business reporter of your local newspaper** and ask him or her which companies in your chosen field are growing and hiring.

- **Call a commercial loan officer with your local bank.** Ask him or her which of the bank's customer companies are growing. Get referrals to key people as well as to other loan officers, accountants and lawyers.

- **Visit or work in nearby restaurants during lunch** to meet employees who can tell you which divisions of their companies are growing and need people.

Improve Your Prospects in a Tight Job Market

Try these approaches for dealing with a slow-growth job market.

Offer to Work for Minimum Wage

If you like a company or want to enter a particular field, offer to work for minimum wage. Make sure the job provides the experience you need. Once you are in the company, you will make friends who can help you move to a better job when it becomes available. And, you will have an insider's advantage.

Free-Lance as a Part-Timer

Working part-time offers experience with flexibility. It helps build personal networks and may even lead to a full-time job. You can use temporary services or look for work on your own. Temp firms offer more opportunities, but for lower pay. Working part-time on your own means you have to find your own work, but the hourly rates are usually higher.

Continue Your Education

Combine academic study with a paid job. Co-op education is a good transition from school to work. If you need a new major or graduate degree for marketability, a co-op is an ideal solution. You get both education and experience. Check with any college or university regarding co-op opportunities.

Try Internships

Normally, internships are ideal for students. However, as a graduate, you may be better qualified for the slot. The contacts and experience you gain are extremely valuable, even if the internship is unpaid. Trade and professional organizations are a good source of internship leads.

Turn Entrepreneur

If you don't really want to work in an office or for someone else and you have a good idea, why not go into business for yourself? Turn a hobby or summer job experience into a money-making venture. It takes little capital to start a service business. You might be able to borrow from your family to start a venture like catering, desktop publishing or home remodeling. And, while prospecting for customers, you will probably get actual job leads. Then you may have some interesting decisions to make about working for someone else versus working for yourself.

Janet Reno, U.S. attorney general, has a bachelor of science degree in chemistry from Cornell University.

How to Use Your Job Prospect Profile

For each person you call or write, start a job Prospect File. Use this form to record all pertinent information about the jobs you're applying for. Make multiple copies of this form and use a separate form for

Job Prospect Profile

Company Name	_____	
Primary Contact	_____	**Title** _____
Telephone	_____	**Secretary** _____
Address	_____	
	_____	
	_____	
Job Title	_____	
Job Responsibilities	_____	
	_____	
Job Qualifications	_____	
	_____	
	_____	
Company Mission	_____	
	_____	
Products/Services	_____	
	_____	
Other Key Contacts	_____	
	_____	
Referred by	_____	
Résumé Sent to	_____	**Date** _____
Follow-Up Call	_____	**Date** _____
Interview (1) With	_____	**Date** _____
Thank-You Note Sent	_____	**Date** _____
Interview (2) With	_____	**Date** _____
Thank-You Note Sent	_____	**Date** _____
Interview (3) With	_____	**Date** _____
Thank-You Note Sent	_____	**Date** _____
Job Offer	_____	**Date** _____

each position. File them alphabetically (by the first initial of each primary contact's last name) after the appropriate Action Log sheet (see page 89). Or, file them in individual folders labeled with the name of the primary contact and company name.

References

If you can, find out where the company banks, what firm does its accounting, who represents it legally and who its customers are, and then check out the company.

Record your feedback here. (For more on this, see the discussion of corporate culture on page 127.)

Commercial bank _____

Accounting firm _____

Law firm _____

Customers _____

_____

Materials Obtained

❏ Annual report ❏ Newspaper stories

❏ Newsletter ❏ Organization chart

❏ Brochures ❏ Telephone directory

❏ Magazine articles ❏ Press kit

Your Own Thoughts

_____

_____

_____

_____

Attach Business Card Here

PART SEVEN

INTERVIEW FOR FIRST PLACE

YOU CAN MASTER THE PROCESS

The objective of the interview is to convince the interviewer that you are the most qualified potential team member. First place gets the job. Second place provides experience that builds character. Here are some guidelines and tactics you can use to win:

Pre-Interview Preparation

- **When scheduling an appointment for an interview,** you should ask to receive information about the job and the company if you have not already done so. Better yet, go pick it up yourself, get a good look at the place and meet the secretary. Ask for annual reports, brochures, a press kit (which includes company history, key personnel, biographies, and product/service information), and especially the job description. This will help you prepare and separate you from the competitors.

- **Ask for directions and how long it will take to get there.** Allow ample time for travel. Arrive twenty minutes early. Don't be sabotaged by unexpected traffic. Wait fifteen minutes outside and review your notes, then walk up to the receptionist five minutes early.

- **Read the information and prepare a 30- to 40-word statement**—your "infomercial"—covering who you are, what your job goal is, and two or three reasons why your skills fit the job requirements. For example: "I've just graduated from Virginia Commonwealth University with a BA in English. My goal is to work as a staff writer with a company like yours. My interest and experience in proposal and report writing for the EPA matches your company's environmental business."

Psyched Out

In 1996, the average salary offer to students receiving doctoral degrees in psychology was $33,078, while the average offer to students receiving bachelor's degrees in chemical engineering was $42,443.

Arsenio Hall, comedian, actor and former talk show host, earned a bachelor's degree in general speech from Kent State University.

Jay Leno, comedian and talk show host, earned his bachelor's degree in speech therapy at Emerson College in Boston.

- **Practice saying your self-description aloud.** Use a tape recorder and listen to how you sound. Are you enthusiastic? Too serious? Does your voice shake?

- **Think about how the interview might go.** Prepare your questions and your responses to the hard questions you anticipate. Repeat this process until you are confident and as prepared as you can be.

- **Videotape practice interviews with friends** who have had successful interviews and can offer tips. If a VCR is not available, practice in front of a mirror.

- **Never turn down an interview.** Interviewing is a skill that you can improve, but practice interviewing is no substitute for the real thing. In addition, an interview can produce referrals.

When You Arrive for the Interview

- **Be friendly to the receptionist.** The interviewer may ask for his or her impression of you. If it is policy to fill out an application, do so even if you already have a résumé. Most firms are required to obtain a standard job application from every applicant.

- **If you're interviewing with a woman,** ask the receptionist beforehand what title—Miss, Ms. or Mrs.—the interviewer prefers.

- **While you are waiting for the interviewer,** peruse one of the magazines that are on the coffee table, or read the newspaper. Don't pull out a novel from your briefcase (unless you're interviewing with a publisher or other creative organization—the book might prompt an interesting discussion that you and the interviewer might benefit from). It's fine to read a book at an airport, but in an interview setting, it often is out of place. It's better to show interest in business, current events or the industry.

- **When the interviewer comes to greet you,** smile broadly, offer a firm handshake and address him or her formally—Mr. Smith, Ms. Jones or Mrs. Green. Practice handshaking with your friends and avoid a limp handshake. A simple thing like a weak handshake can get the interview off to a poor start.

Interview to Win

- **The objective** of the interview is to convince the interviewer that you are the most qualified potential team member.

- **Do your homework.** Reading a company's annual report, brochures, newsletters and job description beforehand will make you an informed candidate.

- **"Tell me about yourself,"** is the way that interviewers almost always begin. It's best to answer this question *after* the job has been described to you so that you can tailor your response accordingly. If you have to talk first, present your prepared self-description.

- **Put yourself in the interviewer's shoes;** listen and try to respond from his or her perspective.

- **If the interviewer tries to engage you in a debate,** say you're not knowledgeable enough about the subject to discuss it.

- **If the interviewer tries to antagonize you,** be as charming and polite as possible. Maintain control and wrestle with the issues, not your emotions.

- **If your interviewer is shy, distracted or unprepared,** you will have to take control of the interview. Talk about your skills and experience and how they relate to the job you're interviewing for. Ask questions (see page 123, "Interview the Interviewer").

Nancy Wexler, a clinical psychologist who helped pinpoint the gene causing Huntington's disease, holds a bachelor's degree in social relations and English from Radcliffe College.

Danny DeVito, actor and director, parked cars for two years.

Bruce Willis, actor, drove work crews around in a truck at a DuPont plant.

- **If the interviewer raises an area of personal interest,** say sports or music, then you should talk sports or music if you wish. Follow his or her lead, and don't attempt to show you know more than he or she does about the subject.

- **Prove you are capable of performing rather than merely describing.** Provide examples and illustrations of what you have accomplished. For example, merely stating that you are good at selling won't get you the job. Prove to the interviewer that you can sell by selling the benefits you offer for this job. Talk about your sales successes.

- **If you are overqualified for the job,** you can state that you are willing to start at the bottom and work your way up. For example, you may be qualified to be a sales representative, but you may have to start as a sales administrator, handling telephone calls and paperwork until a sales representative position is available to you.

- **If you do not understand the question, say:** "I'm sorry, I don't understand the question." Or, "Could you please rephrase the question?"

- **Do not fabricate, guess or generalize,** and do not engage the interviewer in a debate.

- **Do not say why the job would be good or bad for you personally.** That is not the point during the interview. The point is to emphasize how you can help the company.

- **Do not talk yourself out of the job by rambling.** Be brief, be right, then be quiet.

- **At the conclusion of the interview,** indicate that you would love to work for the company if that is what you think and feel.

Post-Interview Actions

- **Send a note thanking the interviewer** for his or her consideration, expressing your interest in the job and reminding the interviewer how well your qualifications fit the position.

- **Attach your interview notes to your Job Prospect Profile** (see pages 106–107) and place them in your job-search organizing notebook or in a folder with the name of the interviewer and company on the tab.

- **Prepare a list of positives and negatives** that will help you make a decision if you receive an offer (see page 138).

- **Call the interviewer** if you have not received a response when one is expected.

Suggested Reading

- *Preparing for Your Interview*
  Diane Berk, Crisp Publications

- *Sweaty Palms: The Neglected Art of Being Interviewed*
  H. Anthony Medley, Ten Speed Press

- *Job Interviews: How to Win the Offer*
  Joyce Lain Kennedy, Sun Features

- *The Perfect Interview*
  John D. Drake, AMACOM

Mario Van Peebles, actor and director of the movie New Jack City, *earned a bachelor's degree in economics from Columbia University. In his first job, he worked as a budget analyst for the New York City Department of Environmental Protection.*

Sample Interview Thank-You Letter

Virginia C. Union
2323 Sullivan Ballou Avenue
Bull Run, VA 22090
(703) 555–1234

July 20, 1997

Ms. Jill Senate
Director of Communications
Washington Associates, Inc.
1801 Pennsylvania Avenue, N.W.
Washington, DC 20000

Dear Ms. Senate:

Thank you for the opportunity to discuss the possibility of joining your organization as a staff writer. Our discussion was helpful in showing how well my English degree, word processing skills and writing experience fit the position.

My specific experience in writing proposals and reports for EPA would be beneficial for your new wetlands project. And, I would enjoy working with your staff on the project.

I appreciate the time you spent with me and look forward to hearing from you. In the meantime, thank you for your consideration.

Sincerely,

Virginia C. Union

Pointers to Increase Your Comfort

Your interview is a conversation between two people who are trying to get to know each other. Here are some tips to make it easier for both of you.

- **Take a note pad with you.** Have a few key points and some important questions already written down. The information will be available to you as you take notes.

- **Maintain good posture.** Sit comfortably, but lean slightly forward to look alert. Smile!

- **Don't sit there like a lump on a log.** Use natural gestures, which will make you appear enthusiastic.

- **Pay attention.** Maintain eye contact, but don't get into a staring contest. Listen attentively.

- **Do not smoke, chew gum, fidget or babble.**

- **Be friendly.** Establish a rapport with the interviewer to make the process easier for the two of you.

- **Be likable.** Try to relate to your interviewer and to what he or she is saying.

- **Be courteous.** Feel free to compliment your interviewer when he or she asks good questions or makes valid points.

- **Never interrupt the interviewer.** Don't finish his or her sentences.

- **Avoid "yes" and "no" answers.** Strike a balance. Show you know what you are talking about, but don't go on forever.

- **Ask good questions.** Base your questions on what you learned from your research.

- **Avoid getting drawn into a discussion of controversial topics.** If the discussion could be pertinent to the job, be diplomatic.

- **Do not criticize anyone or anything.**

What Employers Want

The ideal employee—at any level—is highly motivated, uses common sense, pays attention to detail, can anticipate and solve problems, and is a team player. The following list adds up to a profile of a desirable employee. These are all qualities you can assess in yourself even if you've worked only as a student or as a volunteer.

- **Asks** good questions.

- **Communicates** clearly.

- **Demonstrates** good technical skills.

- **Shows** intelligence and initiative.

- **Follows** instructions.

- **Meets** deadlines.

- **Is self-sufficient** yet contributes as a team member.

- **Handles** details while possessing an overall perspective.

- **Alters** plans flexibly when required.

- **Anticipates** and solves problems diplomatically.

- **Sets** a good example for others.

- **Displays** courtesy, charm and character.

- **Values** accomplishment rather than activity.

- **Does the right things** right the first time.

Questions You May Be Asked

Tell me about yourself. How would you describe yourself?

Present your "infomercial." You may then add information regarding your early years, extracurricular activities and summer or part-time jobs in response to a specific inquiry.

Who are your heroes?

This is an attempt to get to know you better. Have one person in mind with a story that highlights your interests and strengths.

What are your career goals?

You will know your answers based on your reading of Part One. Now relate your answer to the job opportunity you are discussing.

What do you like doing the most?

Relate your response to the situation you are discussing. You may mention an avocation, but don't get trapped into talking about vacationing or socializing.

Describe your most rewarding experience.

Keep your response oriented to the current situation.

How did you like living in (home town)?

Describe the benefits of a small or large community.

Why did you attend (name) college?

State your reasons, such as size, available major, cost, for your decision.

Why did you major in (name)?

Relate your major to your interests and skills.

How much of your college education did you pay for yourself?

This is an opportunity to score big time by giving a percentage figure and then listing scholarships, co-ops, part-time jobs, internships, and summer jobs related to the job for which you are interviewing and that provided the funds for your education. If your parents paid for everything, emphasize what you have done on your own—volunteer work or community service.

(continued)

Questions You May Be Asked (cont'd.)

How did you get involved in (extracurricular activity)?

Tell how you became interested in the activity, then attempt to link it to one of the job requirements or desired personal traits.

Describe the ideal job for you.

Describe the job situation you are discussing in your own words. Don't parrot the exact job description or you will be perceived as uninspired or uninterested.

What are your greatest strengths or weaknesses?

Match one or two strengths to the job requirement. Regarding weaknesses, be honest but turn a negative into a positive. For example, you might say, "In school I tended to procrastinate at times. But, you know, I enjoyed working under the resulting pressure. And I always meet deadlines."

How did you learn of our company?

State the referral, job listing or advertisement or your own research that resulted in the interview.

What do you know about the company?

Based on your preparation, you'll know about its products/services, history, reputation, large customers, growth and profitability.

Why do you want to work for us?

Describe how you can make a contribution to meeting company goals.

What appeals to you about the job?

Describe two or three factors that are attractive to you.

Tell me about your previous job experience.

Be specific in terms of your accomplishments in summer, part-time or full-time jobs. Include volunteer or club experience and any other activity that relates to the situation you are discussing.

Why should we hire you?

Match the benefits from your education, skills and experience to the job requirements.

How do you handle pressure?

Tell the interviewer you enjoy working under pressure. (Remember, deadlines produce results.)

What about working evenings and weekends?

If you can do so honestly, tell the interviewer that you believe in doing what it takes to get the job done efficiently and in a timely fashion.

If you have real limits on your time, say so, and live with the consequences. Be honest with yourself and your employer. If you don't want to work 70 hours a week, don't take a job that you think will require that much overtime.

Are you able to travel? Can you relocate?

Be honest.

What are your salary requirements?

Answer with a question, "What is the salary range for this position?" If no range exists, implement what you will have learned on page 129.

What other jobs are you considering?

Keep your answer related to this field or type of job, and don't be too specific.

May I have a list of references?

Provide references related to your work experience. One academic reference will be adequate.

Is there anything more you would like to know?

Use this opportunity to clarify any issues or to make any points you wish to make that may not have been discussed. Be curious, and show your interest.

Linda Bloodworth-Thompson, creator of sitcoms Designing Women and Evening Shade, was an English teacher in an inner-city high school in Los Angeles.

Diane English, creator of the sitcom Murphy Brown, majored in education at Buffalo State College and taught at an inner-city high school after college.

QUESTIONS THAT YOU SHOULDN'T BE ASKED

In many situations, it is against the law for any employer to invade your privacy. But many times employers *do* ask illegal questions, directly or indirectly. Those include:

- How old are you?

- How is your health?

- What is your marital status?

- What is your religion?

- Do you plan to have children?

- What happens if your spouse gets transferred?

You may also encounter questions or comments that seem inappropriate or make you feel uneasy. For example, an interviewer might compliment you or remark upon your appearance to a degree you're uncomfortable with.

It is important to note that certain employers, like churches, can ask your religious affiliation because the position may entail promoting a specific religion. However, unlawful questions are sometimes asked accidentally.

Assuming that the question is improper, what should you do? Probably the worst thing to do would be to respond angrily that the interviewer's question is illegal. The rapport you may have shared with the interviewer until that moment will be undoubtedly shattered. On the other hand, pay attention to such caution lights. Do you really want to work for a person or company that raises these questions? Regardless, maintain a polite manner. You don't want to burn any bridges. You can do any of the following:

- **Answer the question tactfully** if you want to.

- **Inquire: "Why do you ask?"**

- **Try returning to a discussion of qualifications** by asking: "Could you tell me how this is related to job performance?" or by saying politely: "I'm not clear on how this is pertinent to the job function."

- **Try humor.** If asked about age, you could say: "Put it this way. I haven't been carded lately!" Or, about religion: "I belong to the church of hard work!"

Many women in their twenties and thirties are often asked in interviews whether they are planning to have children soon. If asked this question, you may say, "no." You can always change your mind. And, there are always unplanned pregnancies. When one young woman was asked this question, she responded that children weren't in her plans for a couple of years and that when and if she had children, she intended to get full-time help. That comment immediately satisfied the interviewer, and she got the job.

You should never lie. However, when people illegally pry into your personal life, you do not owe it to them to disqualify yourself. You can always be vague without lying. Never feel obligated to say something you don't want to say.

What If I Have a Disability?

The Americans With Disabilities Act (ADA) states that an employer with 25 or more employees cannot discriminate against a qualified prospective employee with a known disability. The ADA also states that upon hiring the disabled individual, the employer must provide reasonable accommodation, unless undue hardship would result.

Gloria Naylor, author of The Women of Brewster Place, *was a Jehovah's Witness missionary after high school and briefly studied nursing at Medgar Evers College before switching to literature.*

Dave Brubeck,
pianist and
composer, changed
his major from
veterinary medicine
to music while
attending the College
of the Pacific.

This means that if your disability is obvious, interview questions must be posed in terms of your ability to perform essential job functions. In addition, no questions can be asked about prior claims for worker's compensation. Finally, no pre-offer medical exam can be required, and a post-offer exam can be required only if it is required for all employees.

However, you should be aware of two issues. First, you have the responsibility to inform any employer of your disability. Second, an employer can require documentation of your disability.

The key issue during an interview is to keep the focus on your ability to perform essential job functions. It is critical to match your skills with the requirements stated in the job description. As always, straightforwardness and humor are the best approaches. The reality is, regardless of what the law says, you will still have to convince your potential employer that you can do the job. Chances are you can do it better than many people.

INTERVIEW THE INTERVIEWER

Remember, ours is a society of choices. You have a choice of employer. You are looking for a good fit—or chemistry—with the interviewer and a compatibility with the company's culture. The interviewer represents the company. Would you like to work with this person? Why? Why not? You also need to assess:

- **Does the interviewer seem to be acting like himself** or is he playing the "boss" role? Is he representing his company well?

- **Is the company's management style** formal or informal? Is it hands-on or distant? People, numbers or technically oriented? Intense or laid-back?

First impressions count. It is okay to be skeptical. Sometimes the most dumb-sounding questions are the most profound. So don't worry about looking foolish. If you have a question, ask it in a positive way.

Also, listen carefully, observe closely and remember the acronym **GIVE**, described in the box below.

Majors in Demand

In 1996, graduates with bachelor's degrees in the following disciplines enjoyed the highest percentage increases in average salary offers over the year before:

journalism	*+14.9%*
merchandising marketing	*+14.6%*
physical therapy	*+13.9%*

The Meaning of GIVE

Goals
Are the company's and your personal goals aligned? How does the company treat its employees? Does it offer continuing education programs?

Integrity
Can you trust these people? Are they open or secretive? Do they deal in half-truths?

Values
Are the company's beliefs compatible with yours? Is action encouraged? Do employees receive feedback? Does the company promote from within?

Ethics
Will your employer encourage you to break the rules? Is the interviewer asking questions he or she should not be asking? Is there high employee turnover? Why?

Twenty Good Questions to Ask the Interviewer

You will be judged by your questions as well as by your answers. Here are twenty good questions to ask:

1. **May I take notes?**

2. **How did you get started in the company?** What made you successful?

3. **How would you describe the company's business** focus, mission, or goals?

4. **What are the trends** in revenues and profits?

5. **Who are the company's major competitors,** and what are the company's competitive strengths?

6. **Where is the company going** in the next three to five years?

7. **How would you describe the corporate culture?**

8. **What are the specific responsibilities** of the job?

9. **What qualities** would the ideal candidate have?

10. **What would you expect of me** in this position?

11. **How do you see this job evolving?**

12. **Is this a new position** or has the job been held by someone else? If the latter is so, is the person still with the company?

13. **What about others who started in this position** over the past few years? Have any of them been promoted? Into what positions?

14. **Where can this job lead** for a top performer?

15. **What resources are available** to perform this job?

16. **How will I be evaluated?** By whom? When?

17. **What education and training programs** does the company provide?

18. **How will the final hiring decision be made?** By whom? When?

19. **Is there anything else I need to know?**

20. **If you want the job, say:** "I am very interested in this position. What is the next step?"

Close by thanking the interviewer for the opportunity to discuss the situation.

Five Deadly Questions

The following questions will kill your chances of getting the job:

1. What is my salary?

Don't ask about salary unless the interviewer raises the subject first. This may not happen until the second interview or even later, say, when an offer is extended. As curious as you may be, you must be patient or risk leaving the impression that you're more interested in money than in being a team player.

2. How much vacation and sick leave will I get?

Asking about these makes you seem as though you are asking for time off before you have even started the job. Some interviewers may perceive this as a sign of lack of dedication, however unfairly. Naturally, you want to get this information. However, the best way to do it is by asking for a copy of the personnel manual, by talking to the personnel administrator, or by speaking with other employees before taking the job. You should be briefed on benefits at the appropriate time. If not, just ask, "What about the benefits?" after the salary issue has been brought up.

3. How big is my office?

A dedicated team player produces good work regardless of the office environment. Questions regarding office size may be seen as a concern about job appearance rather than the essential elements of the job. Usually, during a tour of the operation, you will be shown the area where you will work.

4. When will I be promoted?

This question is impossible to answer. Promotion depends on timing and your performance. Opportunities for promotion depend on change, such as growth and turnover. Your suitability for promotion depends on your prior performance together with your abilities to plan, organize and get others to perform. Questions regarding promotion should focus on opportunities for advancement, rather than on a commitment that cannot be given.

5. Any negative question!

Any question that is negative or solicits a negative response places the interviewer in an unfavorable and sometimes awkward position. In addition, it makes you look like a negative person. Ask all questions in a positive manner.

WHAT ABOUT THIS CORPORATE CULTURE THING?

To many of us, corporate culture is a vague term. What does it mean? And, why is it relevant to your job search?

Corporate culture is the set of beliefs, traits and values that a company practices over time. Some companies are caring, others are challenging. Some focus on customer service while others value product quality first. In most cases, management has created and nurtured the culture in its own image. In other cases, corporate culture is just pure propaganda.

For your job search, you want to know two things:

- **Is the corporate culture real?** Does the company practice what it preaches?

- **Do you want to join the club?** Can you embrace the culture as your own? Can you function effectively within it? As a member of its team? Do you fit in?

Here's how to find out.

Listen for key claims and slogans.
Some examples include:

- Excellence

- Empowerment

- Open-book management

- Total quality management

Be observant.
You can get a good sense of a company's corporate culture by paying attention to the office environment and what goes on around you while you are interviewing at the company. Look and listen for

Majors in Demand

In 1996, graduates with bachelor's degrees in the following disciplines encountered the greatest percentage decreases in average salary offers compared with the year before:

bioengineering and bio-medical engineering	**-7.3%**
natural resources	**-5.6%**
physics	**-4.7%**

Bennett Cohen, co-founder of Ben & Jerry's Ice Cream, attended several universities including Colgate, Skidmore and the University Without Walls, where his studies included pottery, jewelry making and ceramics.

hints in the elevator, cafeteria and parking lot. Ask yourself the following questions:

- How are you treated by the receptionist?

- Is the office clean, neat and organized?

- How do people dress?

- Are the employees busy?

- Are employees gossiping about one another?

- Is there a spirit of teamwork?

- Are the company's executives accessible to everyone?

- Is the atmosphere formal or informal?

In the interview, ask how the company does things:

- How is work delegated?

- How are decisions made?

- Who has authority to sign for what?

- How are employees rewarded for a job well done?

- Does the company promote from within?

- How do you learn about company news?

Check outside the company.

Independent sources are always worthwhile when checking out a company's corporate culture. Trade associations, chambers of commerce, local business reporters, bankers, public accountants and lawyers can be very helpful. In addition, customers, suppliers and former employees can provide valuable insight into the real culture of an organization. Ask about the company's reputation as an employer. Compare your findings from external sources with what you were told by the interviewer.

SALARY NEGOTIATIONS

Most companies have a salary range for each job. Your ability to negotiate within that range depends on your qualifications together with the salary information you have learned from doing your homework. There is no substitute for knowing the facts and using them for your benefit. Here are some effective ways to deal with the salary issues.

What do you do when the interviewer asks difficult questions like these:

- Have you thought about salary?

- What are your salary requirements?

- What is the minimum salary you will accept?

The best approach, if possible, is to reverse the issue by answering the question with a question. Your response might be:

- "What is the salary range for this position?"

- "Most of my peers who are also graduating with business majors have been receiving offers in the $20,000 to $24,000 range. What range is authorized for this position?"

Be prepared:

- **Have a salary figure in mind** based on the pricing issues discussed in Part Five, "When You Market Yourself."

- **When completing an application,** under "salary required" always write in "negotiable" or "competitive."

Jerry Greenfield, co-founder of Ben & Jerry's Ice Cream, was a pre-med student at Oberlin College, but couldn't get into medical school.

Faye Wattleton, author and former president of the Planned Parenthood, earned a bachelor's in nursing from Ohio State University and a master's in maternal and infant health care from Columbia University, with a specialty in midwifery.

When you're ready to negotiate:

- **Equate your salary requirement to something substantive,** such as a survey, other offers you have received or an explanation of why you require what you're asking.

- **Do not comment immediately on the offer.** It may be the lowest the company can offer. Silence sets the stage for negotiation.

- **Focus on the smallest difference between your figure and the offer**—$20,000 versus $22,000 is about 96 cents an hour. Present the 96 cents difference rather than the $2,000 difference; you're going for the maximum amount presented as a modest increase.

- **Be prepared to split the difference** fifty-fifty as the final resolution. Both parties win.

- **Do not accept a settlement on the spot.** Always ask to sleep on it for a day or two. The company may increase the offer.

- **Do not negotiate benefits in lieu of salary.** Get the salary first. Then deal with the non-salary issues.

Suggested Reading

- *Dynamite Salary Negotiations*
  Ron and Caryl Krannich, PhD's, Impact Publications

- *Getting to Yes*
  Roger Fisher and William Ury, Penguin Books

INTERVIEW DRESS FOR MEN

People make judgments within the first five minutes of an interview. If you appear well-groomed and polished, you will make a good first impression.

A solid or pin-striped gray or navy suit is always a good investment. However, if your budget doesn't allow you to buy a suit, wear a navy blazer and gray trousers. In general, dress above what the job requires. Consider colors you look good in. Avoid herringbone or tiny plaids, which tend to "dance" in the eyes of some people.

Remember to wear a cotton undershirt with your shirt, even in hot weather (it makes the shirt look whiter). Take your shirts to a commercial laundry or dry cleaner and ask for starch (they come out looking much better than you could do at home). Put on a fresh shirt from the cleaners just before the interview. Check your shirt to see whether it needs pressing, and keep your shoes freshly shined. Also:

- **Wear long socks** so no skin will show when you cross your legs.

- **If you wear suspenders,** don't also wear a belt. The suspenders should match or complement your tie. It will be easier to coordinate suspenders and ties if the suspenders are solid or striped (burgundy/navy or red/navy).

- **The tie** should be silk and either striped, paisley or have a small pattern, such as dots. Avoid large, elaborate patterns or ties with too many colors.

- **Get a haircut** or wear a style appropriate to the work situation you're interested in. For example, a ponytail that might be appropriate at some advertising agencies or radio stations might not be appropriate in a law office.

Retired General Colin Powell, former Chairman of the Joint Chiefs of Staff, earned a bachelor's degree in geology at the City College of New York.

Progress

Between 1991 and 1995, salaries for women with four or more years of college increased 10% after accounting for inflation.

- **Leave your earring at home,** unless you're confident about the work situation.

- **Don't wear the exact same outfit** twice to the same company. At least change your tie. Make note of what you wear to each interview on your Action Log or Job Prospect Profile.

INTERVIEW DRESS FOR WOMEN

Remember that one's dress and grooming send out powerful messages to a prospective employer. If you want to be absolutely appropriate in most corporate settings, choose a classic suit in navy, gray or black (or a lighter neutral in summer or warmer climates). A conservative dress with a jacket would also work provided it is not too low cut, girlish or bright. Although a suit or dress is preferable, a navy blazer and classic gray skirt (wool in winter, linen in summer) can be worn. Make sure you choose a suit with a classic cut that fits well. If necessary, take the suit to a tailor for alterations. On no occasion should you wear pants. As for the blouse, keep it simple, subdued and jewel-necked in a natural-looking fabric.

- **Shorter skirts are acceptable,** provided that the skirt meets the top of the knee. Do not interview in a short skirt unless you are looking for a position with a company that makes or sells short skirts.

- **Clinging clothes, flashy or glittery fingernails,** open-toe shoes and dangling earrings are all inappropriate for an interview. Get a good haircut, and if your hair tends to look a little wild, wear it up, back or with a headband. If you wear nail polish, make sure none of the polish is chipped and that the color is either clear or pale pink.

- **Wear just a few pieces of jewelry.** Stud earrings, watch, pearls and one gold chain are sufficient. Don't wear more than one ring on each hand. Pearl studs and a strand of pearls can add a classic touch.

- **Pantyhose,** even in the summer, are a must. Bare legs might escape the attention of a male interviewer, but the odds are that any woman who interviews you would notice. It's a good idea to carry a spare pair in your briefcase or purse.

- **Briefcases are optional,** but find one proportional to your size or you'll look like you're carrying your Dad's. What you should avoid, however, is carrying a tote or shopping bag to the interview. If you need to wear athletic shoes en route to the interview, carry a briefcase large enough to conceal them. Change into your pumps outside the building. You will be less nervous doing this away from the gaze of the company receptionist, and you can concentrate on observing the company employees and the office atmosphere.

- **Don't wear the exact same outfit** twice to the same company. At least wear a different blouse or other accessories. Make note of what you wear to each interview on your Action Log or Job Prospect Profile.

Remember, how you apply this advice will depend on the place of employment, type of business and part of the country, including the city. A woman applying for a graphic design, architecture, ad agency, retail or other creative position may have more leeway with the way she dresses and may need to use it.

But It's Still Less

Overall in 1995, women earned 76 cents for every dollar earned by men. That's up from 70 cents in 1991.

*David Geffen, media
mogul, flunked out of
the University of
Texas and Brooklyn
College.*

You Can Obtain Value From Each Interview

Rejection letters are inevitable. Do not take them personally. Most of the time, there was a better candidate for the job. However, you can use the situation to obtain suggestions for improvement and referrals.

Obtain some real value from each rejection letter. Don't let a simple "no" affect you in a negative way. Call each person who has sent a rejection letter and thank him or her for considering you. Ask for suggestions for improving your résumé, interview skills or job-search direction. Write the suggestions on the Job-Search Improvement Suggestions form on the next page.

Remember to ask for referrals to other organizations or people who might be able to use your abilities or capabilities. Try to obtain two or three leads.

Finally, ask what the person would do if he or she were in your situation. Who would he or she call? Above all, never, never, never give up. Keep calling. Keep learning. Keep improving. You will be successful.

Suggested Reading

- *The Complete Job Interviewing Handbook*
  John J. Marcus, Harper Perennial

Ways to Improve Your Job Campaign

The farther you progress in your job campaign, the more you will discover what works and what doesn't. Take the time to evaluate your job-search techniques and use this worksheet to jot down how you can strengthen your strategy. Keep multiple copies in your job-search organizing notebook and consider filling it out weekly and/or after each job interview.

Modify Strategy or Tactics

_____

_____

_____

Revise Résumé

_____

_____

_____

Acquire New Skills

_____

_____

_____

Improve Interview Techniques

_____

_____

_____

Obtain More Referrals

_____

_____

_____

My Own Thoughts

_____

_____

_____

TIME
TO MAKE
A DECISION

Go or No-Go?

Once you receive an offer, you normally have a short period of time, such as two to three weeks, to respond. In most situations, multiple offers are not received simultaneously. Therefore, each offer must be considered on its own merits.

Your decision is a judgment call. The key is to make the call based on the elements that are important to you: compatibility with your long-term and short-term goals, competency in performing daily tasks, ability to work with your supervisor for mutually beneficial results and comfort with the corporate culture.

If you have serious doubts about an offer, it is best to meet with whomever is making the offer to resolve your doubts. If you can't resolve them, do not accept the offer. Don't fool yourself and waste months or years of your life. On the other hand, don't reject an offer based on trivial concerns, such as not having your own parking space or having to share an office.

Keep compensation and benefits in the proper perspective. Sometimes non-monetary rewards, such as paid educational benefits, are more important than starting salary in the long run. And, there are times when a lower starting salary will be outweighed by near-term promotion opportunities.

Once you have decided for or against a job offer, it is appropriate to extend a written acceptance or refusal to the company that made you the offer. Your letter can be short and to the point, and should always be courteous (see the sample letters on pages 140 and 141).

Bill Cosby, comedian, actor and author, dropped out of the physical education program at Temple University in Philadelphia during his sophomore year. In 1977, he earned his doctoral degree in education from the University of Massachusetts.

JOB OFFER EVALUATION

Scoring an offer will help you analyze the situation. It will not make the decision for you. However, it will provide a structured and consistent approach to thinking about an offer. And, you may modify the list to suit your personal perspective. Also, you may want to review Part One, "Why Will You Work?", regarding career suitability and quality-of-life issues. It, too, will provide a framework for considering an offer.

Make one copy of the form for each prospective employer who extends an offer. File it after the appropriate Job Prospect Profile Worksheet.

On your Evaluation Form, score each item from one (lowest) to ten (highest). The maximum score is 180. Because the scoring is subjective, you can set your own range for consideration. For example, 140 might be the appropriate cut-off for a generous scorer, while 100 might be more reasonable for a critical scorer. Remember, the score does not make the decision, you do.

Evaluation Form

Company Name _____

Primary Contact _____

The Position   *Score*
- How does the position fit with my career goals?   _____
- Will I have meaningful responsibilities that can be measured?   _____
- Will I be visible to key people in the company?   _____
- Do I really want this job?   _____

Your Supervisor
- Can I work with this person?
- Do I respect this person's values?   _____
- Is this person liked and respected by his or her co-workers   _____
  and supervisors?
                                                           _____

The Company
- Is the company growing?
- Is the company profitable?   _____
- How does the company rank compared with its competitors?   _____
- Is there opportunity for advancement?   _____
- Do I fit in?   _____
                                                           _____

Compensation
- Can I live on the salary? If not, can I supplement it with income
  elsewhere and make it a livable salary?   _____
- Are the benefits adequate?   _____
- Are training and educational programs available?   _____

Related Factors
- How easy is commuting?
- How affordable is housing?   _____
- How compatible is the location with my lifestyle?   _____
                                                           _____

                                              Total   _____

My Own Thoughts

_____

_____

_____

_____

RESPONSE TO OFFERS

Once you have decided for or against a job offer, it's appropriate to write a courteous note of acceptance or refusal to the company that made you the offer. Your letter can be short and to the point. Consider the following examples.

Sample Acceptance Letter

Virginia C. Union
2323 Sullivan Ballou Avenue
Bull Run, VA 22090
(703) 555–1234

August 16, 1997

Ms. Jill Senate
Director of Communications
Washington Associates, Inc.
1801 Pennsylvania Avenue, N.W.
Washington, DC 20000

Dear Ms. Senate:

I am pleased to accept your offer to join Washington Associates, Inc., as a staff writer at an annual salary of $20,000. I am confident that my responsibilities will be both interesting and challenging.

I look forward to my new career with Washington Associates and will report to your office at 8:30 A.M. on September 7, 1997, as agreed. Thank you.

Sincerely,

Virginia C. Union

Sample Rejection Letter

Virginia C. Union
2323 Sullivan Ballou Avenue
Bull Run, VA 22090
(703) 555–1234

August 16, 1997

Ms. Jill Senate
Director of Communications
Washington Associates, Inc.
1801 Pennsylvania Avenue, N.W.
Washington, DC 20000

Dear Ms. Senate:

Thank you for your offer to join Washington Associates, Inc., as a staff writer. Unfortunately, I am unable to accept the offer because I have accepted a similar position with another company.

I appreciate the opportunity to be considered for employment with Washington Associates, Inc. Best wishes for your continued success.

Sincerely,

Virginia C. Union

Gary Larson, cartoonist and creator of "The Far Side," earned a bachelor's in communications from Washington State University, while also taking courses in zoology, ornithology, entomology, archeology and anthropology.

TWENTY TIPS FOR SUCCESS IN YOUR FIRST JOB

Congratulations, you've accepted your dream job. You have been hired as a contributing team member. Put the team first, "me" second. As a team member, you will be expected to produce. Anticipate, don't wait for detailed directions. Get ahead of the pack. Beat deadlines. Exceed expectations. Then ask yourself, "How can I do better?"

Beware of office politics. Learn to work within the system and without being manipulated. Deal with the facts—who, what, when, where, how, why—together with your recommendations for solving problem situations. Finally, observe the following proven rules for succeeding on the job.

1. **Be visible.** Introduce yourself to everyone. Relate well to others. Be likeable.

2. **Assume responsibility for your own success.** Don't make excuses.

3. **Accept new risks as opportunities to expand your potential.** Don't be afraid to make a mistake—just don't make the same one twice.

4. **Be willing to pay your dues.** Volunteer with good humor and pleasantness for the tasks no one else wants to do.

5. **Make your supervisor's decision to hire you a good decision.** Hopefully, he or she will become a mentor who can help guide your career development. Always keep your supervisor informed.

6. **Be a productive, pleasant and effective team player.** Try to suggest creative solutions to tough problems.

7. **Learn to observe with a "third eye and ear."** People don't always say what they mean. Observe actions as well as words.

8. **Don't go to meetings unprepared.** Always take notes and highlight those points you want your supervisor to know. Maintain a meetings diary.

9. **Focus on performing your job as best you can.** Don't worry about how others are performing.

10. **Avoid other peoples' problems and miseries.** Don't take sides in personal battles. Deal with the issues, not the personalities or emotions.

11. **Get to work early or leave late.** It's amazing how much you can accomplish without people and telephone interruptions.

12. **Respect other people's values.** Different does not mean inferior. Respect is the foundation for successful relationships.

13. **Learn to separate facts from opinions, issues from feelings.** Focus on defining the problem, then solving it diplomatically.

14. **Negotiate differences of opinion.** Team success depends on mutual agreement. Don't get into "we" versus "they" arguments. Attacking, condemning and fighting leads to team failure.

15. **Take advantage of every educational and training opportunity.** Improve your abilities and learn new skills. Go for consistent personal growth, not instant perfection.

16. **Try to do the right things right the first time.** Then improve your efforts next time—and every time.

Michael Crichton, author of Jurassic Park *and* ER, *which became the basis of the popular television series, has a bachelor's degree in anthropology from Harvard University and is a physician.*

Spike Lee, filmmaker and actor, earned his bachelor's in mass communications at Morehouse College in Atlanta.

17. **Honor your commitments.** Make sure you deliver what you agreed to deliver when you agreed to deliver it—no excuses, ever.

18. **Always set the example.** If you can remember this one rule, everything else will fall into place.

19. **Learn to deal with day-to-day frustrations.** Humor, optimism and confidence help. Build confidence through many small victories.

20. **Have a life away from the office.** Enjoy an avocation to break the work routine. If you play as hard as you work and work as hard as you play, both parts of your life will be fun.

Suggested Reading

- *The Precious Present*
  Spencer Johnson, Doubleday

- *The Seven Habits of Highly Effective People*
  Stephen R. Covey, Simon & Schuster

- *SuccessAbilities!*
  Paula Ancona, Chamisa Press (1–800–WORKTIP)

LOOKING AHEAD

Mary Chapin-Carpenter, country-music songwriter and performer says it best: "My work helps me have an identity, which helps me feel like I have a place, which makes me feel like I have a purpose." Today, Carpenter is branching into writing children's books and is a big supporter of human rights organizations. She keeps expanding her horizons, which is one key to her continuing success.

Compare her situation to many of the thirty-something people I meet who feel trapped in their "dull, boring, miserable" careers or jobs. Most of these people:

- **never determined what they liked or were good at** prior to selecting a college major or a career track,

- **accepted the first or highest-paying job offer** regardless of the things they cared about, and

- **perhaps most importantly, failed to grow**—wherever they were, whatever they were doing, and even if they originally enjoyed their jobs.

So, before looking ahead, take a moment to check and make sure that what you are about to do is interesting, worthwhile and really turns you on.

If you can't pass the turned-on test, what do you do? First, go back to page 21 and read the "Suggested Reading." Second, go to page 18 and take some of the interest, aptitude and personality tests discussed there. Seize control of your life and steer it toward the career you want—and do it now!

If you pass the turned-on test, you are positioned for success, but that's not the end of it. You must keep on growing. The next section will show you how.

Your Career Is Your Business

Like a business, you can't just start up your career and then ignore it. You must manage your career as if it were your own company. A company's first goal is to serve the customer's interests, and on the job, your boss is your customer. Make yourself valuable to that person, and make him or her look good. The 20 tips outlined earlier in this chapter will help you meet that goal.

But successful companies must also grow. They can't rest on their laurels. They constantly reassess what they're doing and how they're doing it. They look for new and better ways to do business and learn as they go. Likewise, in your career you must expand your

Faith Popcorn, marketing trend forecaster and author of the Popcorn Report, *majored in theater at New York University.*

options. You must continually reinvent yourself. These tips will help:

Take care of your employees.

You are the sole employee. Set goals and reward yourself for meeting those goals. Every month, reassess your goals: Are you still working toward them? Have you achieved them? Have they changed? Do you need to set new ones?

Build your business.

Network with a purpose. Make everyone else better by working with you. Be desirable to work with. Produce good results. Share the credit for mutual success. These strategies will generate new opportunities.

Take risks.

Expand your interests. Volunteer for jobs no one else wants. Dare to work harder and smarter than your peers at work.

Take time to learn something new each week.

Just doing a good job is no longer a guarantee of continued employment. You must develop an area of expertise that makes you indispensable.

Combine marketable skills to become indispensable.

Blending diverse but complementary disciplines can make your services more valuable, and that means you can charge more for them. For example, you could combine:

- journalism with educational technology

- engineering with project management

- philosophy with computer science

- nursing with public administration

- English with World Wide Web technology

- information science with an MBA

- technical communications with human communications, and

- any field with corporate etiquette or public speaking

Embrace technology.

Today's world is driven by information. Timely access to information requires technology. The better you use technology, the more likely you are to be successful in any field. Stay current; there will always be something new to learn.

Become an expert communicator.

Being a good writer and speaker gives you a competitive edge. Take courses in business communications and public speaking. Always make your words count—even in e-mail.

Think globally.

More and more companies are doing business abroad, so it's smart to learn a new language or about a new culture. Cultural and language skills will differentiate you from your peers.

Be adaptable.

You, like any company, must be able to react to market-driven change. If you can work well in a fast-paced, unstructured environment, you'll find it easier to switch jobs or careers when you need or want to.

Remember, we are all "free agents."

The bottom line is that everyone is in business for him- or herself. When you've done all you can do for your "client" and exhausted all the possibilities, it's time to look for new opportunities elsewhere and move on. You may even end up working for yourself one day.

Mae Jemison, the first black female astronaut, joined the Peace Corps as a doctor.

LIFELONG LEARNING ON THE VIRTUAL CAMPUS

Throughout this book I have encouraged you to acquire new skills, combine complementary disciplines and expand your horizons to keep you marketable long into the 21st century. Maybe you'll want to get the master's degree you need to advance in your career or you'll discover a new and interesting field to explore. If you think limited money or time will keep you from pursuing the knowledge you want, think again. Today, if you have a computer and access to America Online, CompuServe or the Internet, you can take courses in your own home, even in your pajamas if you wish, at a pace and price you can afford.

The Internet offers the most extensive online class offerings. It's accessible via the major online services, but if you plan on taking classes or making extensive use of it, the cheapest access is probably through a national or regional Internet service provider. You should also have a 28.8 K bps modem or faster for the degree of speed necessary for the rapid response you expect.

Here are some of the current options:

The College and Adult Students Forum
CompuServe, goword: stufob

The Forum has lots of offerings, including online courses and degrees available from dozens of colleges and universities, conference and chat rooms, message areas and libraries. For information about courses and degrees, go to "Library" in the top menu.

The Electronic University Network (EUN)
America Online, keyword: EUN
http://www.wcc-eun.com/eun

EUN offers undergraduate and graduate level courses from eight accredited colleges and universities. Coursework usually involves one or more of the following: real-time lectures in which students and teacher interact online, e-mail between you and your instructor, message boards where you can discuss ongoing class work with other enrolled students, and "libraries" to help with assignments. The cost is $59 to $300 per credit hour depending on the school, plus online time. To get a feel for EUN, sign up by e-mail for its free mini course.

Globewide Network Academy (GNA)
http://www.gnacademy.org

GNA is a consortium of educational and research organizations that offers online courses leading to degrees. Its Web site lists more than 400 courses on topics such as art, business, computers, engineering, language, literature and writing. GNA's noncredit courses run from a few dollars up to $100, and credit courses cost about $100 per credit hour. Those fees don't include online time.

UOL Publishing, Inc.
http://www.uol.com

UOL partners with colleges, universities, corporations and associations to offer off-site education via the Internet. For example, Park College in Parkville, Mo., offers business communications and technical writing classes online. Keep in mind that UOL doesn't actually enroll any students, only their partners do. To check out UOL's partner offerings, visit its website.

Virtual Online University
http://www.iac.net/~billp

VOU is a nonprofit corporation offering professional, degree and continuing-education courses from Athena University. Athena is a "virtual" university—it exists online but has no physical location, buildings or classrooms. It is presently working toward accreditation. Students can pursue B.A. and M.A. degrees in liberal arts.

Continuing education courses run from 2 to 13 weeks, usually meeting interactively with the instructor in real time for an hour or two a week. For-credit courses, which typically take 13 weeks, cost about $100 per

Jeff Smith, TV's "Frugal Gourmet," earned a bachelor's degree in philosophy and sociology at the University of Puget Sound and then a master's of divinity from Drew Theological School.

William Hurt, actor, has a bachelor's degree in theology from Tufts University.

credit hour. Noncredit courses are priced according to the length and the amount of teacher involvement online. Neither fee includes online time. You can find out about VOU's classes, orientation sessions, registration and fees at its Web site.

A FINAL WORD OF ADVICE

Now that you've made it through the process of starting or restarting your career, it's time to close the book—but not to throw it away. Be sure to save this volume and the personal job-search organizing notebook that you've created. Keep these resources for that inevitable moment when it's time again to assess your needs, desires and situation and engage in planning, organizing and conducting a job campaign. You'll also have fun looking at this record and realizing how far you have come in your personal and career development.

Remember, too, that your newly developed network of friends, family and acquaintances have real value—now and in the future. They can continue to provide support to you and your endeavors. Just be sure to keep in touch and to reciprocate. And never forgetting how you were helped, volunteer to help others who need your assistance.

Finally, best wishes for many successful careers ahead.

INDEX